FLYING - NOT JUST FOR WHITE GUYS

A HISTORY OF DIVERSITY IN AVIATION AND AEROSPACE

CRAIG S. MARCKWARDT

DEDICATIONS

To my wife Sharyne, who makes me fly, and to my granddaughter
Lilyanne who I trust will grow
to soar even higher

INTRODUCTION AND ACKNOWLEDGEMENTS

I volunteer as a docent and educator at Frontiers of Flight, a Smithsonian affiliated aviation and space museum located at Dallas Love Field. Among the courses that I facilitate is one that has evolved from a basic introduction to aerodynamics and flight into one designed specifically for high school students involved in the Gulfstream Aerospace Corporation Student Leadership Program. These young people are primarily African-American or Hispanic boys and girls whom SLP is attempting to interest in aerospace careers as engineers, pilots, technicians, or manufacturing professionals. The program includes seminars, tours of Gulfstream facilities, and an opportunity for a summer internship with Gulfstream. A few months into Frontiers of Flight's involvement, I was asked to find examples of diversity in aerospace that would allow these students to better identify with the program's goals.

A search among the hundreds of artifacts and exhibits in the museum turned up the following: An exhibit covering Amelia Earhart fairly extensively, a brief mention of the Ninety-Nines, memorabilia related to the Women's Airforce Service Pilots, a captioned poster featuring women's roles in manufacturing during World War II ("Rosie the Riveter"), and several pieces of information on the Tuskegee Airmen. The latter was the only one addressing any role that African-Americans might have had in aviation, while I found nothing involving Hispanics.

With that, my journey began. What follows are the results.

I have a personal interest in this project beyond my scholarly curiosity. First, I have a granddaughter who shows a great propensity toward things scientific, including astronomy and aeronautics, and I want to encourage her as much as I can. Secondly, in obtaining my own pilot certificate my first "discovery flight" just before I retired from the corporate world, all but two hours of my fifty hours of dual instruction, and my final check ride were all carried out by female pilots.

Finally, something that has gnawed at me for years surely kept the burner lit and the pot boiling as I set about trying to find evidence of diversity in aviation. In the mid-1980's a fellow employee, a West Texas native, commenting on probability of something happening said, "That's about as likely as a n***** aviator." And thirty-five years later I believe that I have finally come up with a good response.

It is my hope that this compilation becomes a resource for broadening the curriculum for aerospace studies at Frontiers of Flight, and for any program seeking to overcome the perception flying has always been the purview of only white men. I want for any kid who looks up every time he or she hears the sound of an airplane overhead, or watches a hawk magically circle upward while riding a thermal, or looks at the Moon and wants to be the next person who witnesses Earthrise, to be able to see his- or herself constrained only by the educational and physical hurdles that must be overcome, not by social constraints.

I need to express my deep appreciation to the education staff at Frontiers of Flight, in particular Alicia Morgan, the former Vice President of Education Programs who, as an engineer of African-American heritage, provides a visible role model for my intended audience and an inspiration for my research. I also value the work of Al Wright and the Gulfstream

Aerospace Student Leadership Program whom, I believe, is making a positive difference in the community.

I would like to acknowledge a number of sources of inspiration that I been privileged to have met and learned from while a docent at Frontiers of Flight. Several have, in their own right, been responsible for overcoming bias and discrimination and moving the goalposts for aspiring aviators and engineers today. These include the late Lt. Calvin J. Spann (Tuskegee Airmen), Mary Wallace "Wally" Funk (Mercury 13), and Dr. Christine Darden, Ph.D. (NACA Computer, Hidden Figures).

Thanks, also, for the organization Women in Aviation International who annually bring their inspiration and resources to the young women of the Dallas, Texas area through events at Frontiers of Flight.

I need to acknowledge my granddaughter Lilyanne who provides me with inspiration to leave the world a better place for her then when I found it.

And most importantly, without the love, support and encouragement of my wife of fifty-plus years, Sharyne, I may not have earned my own wings, nor would this book exist.

Craig Marckwardt

FOREWORD

This compilation should, in all likelihood, be spilt into two volumes. Any history of flight will include countless exploits of male aeronauts and aviators, nearly all of Northern European lineage. This even predates the actual accomplishment of flight. Growing up, the first books I read that gave me an encyclopedic overview of aviation that inevitably included the tale of Daedalus and his son Icarus, who fashioned wings from feathers and wax, but came to grief when Icarus flew too close to the Sun. The Aeolipile of Hero of Alexandria was touted as the first reaction engine, a precursor to the Jet Age. And Italy's Leonardo da Vinci, who among his myriad talents, drew up plans for an ornithopter, a helicopter, and a parachute (one of these actually worked).

According to these compendia actual flight begins with the French Montgolfier brothers, and developments in lighter-than-air craft follow on with the German von Zeppelin. Unpowered, winged flight is peppered with English, French and German names like Cayley, Ferber and Lilienthal, until the American Wright brothers figured out the secret of combining thrust and control.

In fact, in the 1950's, as a kid entranced with flight, I did not encounter any mention of anyone who wasn't white and male until the story of Amelia Earhart. As time passed, I was treated to glimpses of the Women's Airforce Service Pilots, mostly as a footnote to the flying aces of World War II. Much later, I became aware of the Tuskegee Airmen but years would pass before I would know the whole story.

Women in flight date to the earliest days of ballooning, and women flying winged, powered airplanes have been around since nearly the beginning of aviation. While women had to go to sometimes extraordinary lengths to be allowed to fly, only by their novelty, were they generally accepted, and acknowledged in the popular media of their respective times.

On the other hand, the involvement of people of color, especially African-Americans, both male and female, travels on a separate but parallel course. Over the years, these paths have touched occasionally, but until recently never merged.

Of course, this follows historical and sociological trends in lockstep. The women who flew were, most often, doing so with equipment supplied by, and with the tutelage of, men. In spite of their best efforts, often outperforming male pilots, women were relegated to "novelty" status. From the first balloon flight of Elisabeth Thible in 1783, to Jackie Cochran's assault on the sound barrier in the early 1950's, there always seemed to be a man involved. Women's participation in daring pursuits, as their moments in time provided context, were thought to be unseemly, scandalous, and unladylike. Of course, as women were liberated from patriarchy in the last half century, or so, all of that has changed.

Well, almost. Only 17% of pilots are female, even today, and news articles abound about "good ol' boy" conditions in the halls of engineering and commercial aviation.

The second track is even more closely tied to the social mores of the time. After the Civil War and Reconstruction, white society failed to embrace the inclusion of people of African descent. Growing up in the 1950's I am sure that I never questioned the status quo, because no one in my immediate life gave segregation, *de jure* or otherwise, a thought. What I didn't see was that, somewhere on the other side of town there existed a parallel universe. It was a self-contained community that mirrored the one in which I lived, but never overlapped with my reality. I grew up in Los Angeles where that other reality was on the south and east side of the city (Watts), but would have been equally so in any big city like New York (Harlem) or Chicago (the South Side). It is that the involvement of African-Americans in aviation occurred with minimal contact with the social majority.

What leads me to tie both of these tales together, as much as anything, are the occasions when things did touch, and sparks were ignited, and little fires burned through the walls of separation. This, then, is a look at the dismantling of racial and gender barriers. And for those efforts, we are all better off.

ABOUT THE AUTHOR

CRAIG S. MARCKWARDT

I am volunteer docent and educator at Frontiers of Flight, the Smithsonian affiliated flight museum located at Dallas Love Field, Texas. In that capacity I provide aerospace-related classes to area youngsters, both in the museum's classroom and gallery facilities, and through outreach in local elementary, middle and high schools.

I am retired from a career in automotive product and customer relations training and development. My former employers include major Tier 1 automotive manufacturers. In that capacity I developed and implemented classroom curricula and support materials as an adult educator.

I grew up in Southern California, and attended California State University, Los Angeles, as a Social and Industrial Psychology major. I have lived in Dallas, Texas, since 1980.

I am a certificated pilot. My deep interest in aviation and aerospace stems from my having been the son of a U.S. Air Force flight engineer in the early 1950's who, stationed at Carswell Air Force Base, Ft. Worth, Texas, flew the 10-engine Convair B-36 "Peacemaker" strategic bomber. My dream of flying as a pilot was realized in 2015, having helped to raise my family and retire from my career.

My interest in social diversity and civil rights developed in Los Angeles in the 1960's. I have a granddaughter for whom gender equality issues hit especially close to home. The vast majority of the students I provide with STEM education are young people of color.

This is my first project of book length. I spent my career developing, writing and implementing educational materials for the aforementioned companies, and continue to do so for Frontiers of Flight. In fact, this project is an extension of subject curricula requested to support the Gulfstream Aerospace Student Leadership Program as they found little historical material addressing the roles of women and people of color in aviation and aerospace. From that seed, the manuscript that is available to you grew from PowerPoint slides and handouts to personal stories of little noticed pioneers.

I can be contacted at:

cmarckwardt@sbcglobal.net

TABLE OF CONTENTS

Chapter 1 - The Aeronauts

The use of heated air as a lifting medium dates back to around the 3rd century. The Chinese built envelopes of oiled rice paper on bamboo frames and used wax candles as a heat source. These *Kongming* lanterns became a staple of Chinese celebrations and are still seen today. Hot air became the stairway to human flight centuries later.

Ask anyone who made the first successful manned flight and the answer will, more often than not, be "The Wright Brothers, of Dayton, Ohio, USA". Ask a French citizen who made the first successful manned light and you might get a different answer. It was a pair of French brothers who first managed to get a person off the ground and return him safely to earth.

Montgolfier Aerostat

In the late 18th century, Paris was the cultural epicenter of the western world. Louis XVI ruled France with Marie Antoinette at his side. To say that the French monarchy led an opulent lifestyle might be considered understatement. The monarchy was given to patronage of artists, scholars and inventors that provided France with a high level of respect and credibility as the seat of learning and civilization. Great Americans, including such notables as Thomas Jefferson and Benjamin Franklin spent time in Paris, in and around the court and courtiers of the emperor. To grasp the magnitude of the French aristocracy one needs only to look at pictures of the Palace of Versailles, its décor and furnishings.

In 1783, five years before the Constitution was ratified creating the United States of America, science was considered a branch of philosophy. The concept of elements comprised of atoms was yet to be formulated. The well-heeled of Europe dressed in fine clothing and sported powdered wigs. Men wore below-the-knee length breeches with stockings and buckle shoes, fancy coats over ruffed blouses, and tricorn hats. Women wore gowns over corsets and petticoats, and in France, both men and women sported facial makeup. Hardly the modern image of the intrepid, adventurous aviator.

Against this background, though, physical science was blossoming. In the New World, prominent people including the aforementioned Franklin and Jefferson were exploring electricity, meteorology, paleontology and botany and looking to find practical uses for these discoveries. In this environment the Montgolfier brothers were experimenting with the use of hot air as a lifting medium, building larger and larger envelopes designed to carry payloads aloft.

The Montgolfier brothers publicly launched their unoccupied hot air balloon *Annonay* for an audience of French dignitaries. This was the first of several over the following few months that established the Montgolfiers as having invented the working flying machine.

A goat named *Patris* became the first "test pilot" to rise off the Earth in a vehicle produced by human ingenuity. In and around Paris, *Les frères* Montgolfier were concerned that separating terrestrial beings from their connection with the ground might prove to be harmful. On September 11 of the same year, for their first public, untethered demonstration of their *globe aérostatique* for King Louis XVI and Marie Antoinette of France, the Montgolfiers launched a crew comprising a duck, a rooster, and a sheep. It was thought that a duck, as it regularly flies, would have no issues, while the rooster who only operates at low altitude might. The greatest concern was for the sheep. After a flight that reached an altitude of about 1500 feet and covered about 3 miles, the intrepid crew returned safely, if not softly, to Earth.

As an interesting side note, in lieu of the aviating animals, it was initially proposed by King Louis that the first flights be done with convicts. That would have made the first aeronauts convicted criminals.

As it happened, the Montgolfier brothers, who were paper manufacturers by trade, built a 75-foot tall, 60,000 cubic foot capacity balloon of cloth and paper, large enough to lift a person. Imagine the sight. The royal blue balloon, as tall as a seven story building, was decorated with golden *fluers-de-lis*, signs of the zodiac, and images of the Sun with King Louis' face in each. Étienne Montgolfier became the first person to lift off the earth in October of 1783. Later that day, a French physicist, Pilâtre de Sara Rozier, became the second, reaching the end of the 80 foot tether. It had to have been magnificent.

The Montgolfiers were convinced that their hot air balloons rose because of a gas created by combustion. Clearly, this was an interesting era for scientific thought and advancement.

On November 21, 1783, de Rozier and the Marquis d'Arlades rose from a chateau on the outskirts of Paris and travelled over 5 miles reaching an altitude of 3000 feet for about 25 minutes above Paris. The duration was limited as the heat required to keep the balloon airborne was found to be singeing the fabric of the balloon. This was the first time that any human being had left the earth, unfettered, and returned safely in a flying machine. This was, also, likely the first time that any human beings had seen any animal aloft that wasn't there as a result of natural selection. A real sight for the citizens of Paris.

Less than two weeks later, a French inventor, Jacques Alexandre César Charles, rose to an altitude of about 10,000 feet in a balloon filled with hydrogen. Hydrogen, then called "inflammable air", was discovered by an Englishman, Henry Cavendish, in 1766. Cavendish developed a method of isolating hydrogen from water using acids and metal as catalysts. He also described the specific weight of hydrogen (as well as noting that the ratio of hydrogen to oxygen in water was 2 to 1) which led to the invention of the lighter-than-air balloon not using heat to produce the required buoyancy.

Hydrogen would go on to become the lifting medium of choice as lighter-than-air flight developed over the following century and a half.

With ballooning becoming more commonplace, demonstrations became more and more daring and aimed at pleasing a crowd. On June 4, 1784, a Monsieur Fleurant "piloted" a Montgolfier balloon accompanied by a 19-year old French opera singer, Elisabeth Thible. Madame Thible was not the first woman to fly in a balloon, but she was the first to fly untethered. The flight, performed to entertain the visiting king of Sweden, Gustave II, lasted 45 minutes, covered about 3 miles and reached 8,500 feet. Mme. Thible, dressed as the goddess Minerva stoked the fire for the heat source, and sang operatic duets with Fluerant during the flight. Although no graphic evidence of this flight seems to remain, I picture Mme. Thible in flowing robes, bearing a shield and spear, and topped with a polished helmet featuring a cockscomb of feathers, Mohawk style.

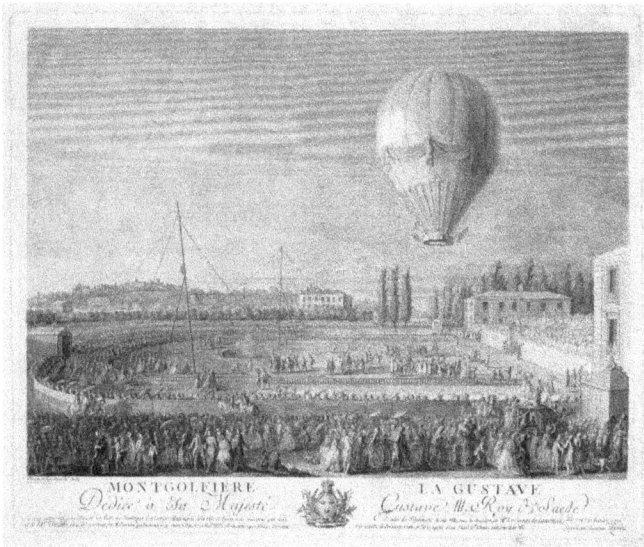

La Gustave

It is recorded that as the balloon, *la Gustave*, descended and touched the ground, the top ripped open and the fabric toppled on the aeronauts. Fleurant used his knife to free himself and sought to rescue his co-pilot, only to find that Mme. Thible was already clear and safe.

Perhaps as interesting is that the original plan called for Count Jean Baptiste de Laurencin to accompany Fleurant. The Count had been a passenger of Joseph Montgolfier on a flight the previous January. That flight ended after 12 minutes when the balloon began to burn and tear. Based on his experience, the Count elected to decline.

As noted, women had flown prior to this in a balloon. On May 20, 1784, the Marchioness and Countess of Montalembert, the Countess of Podenas and a Miss de Lagarde had taken a trip on a tethered balloon in Paris, but Elisabeth Thible was the first woman in the world to float free in a hot air balloon.

Aerial exhibitions continued through the end of the 1700's and into the next century. Andre-Jacques Garnerin was the inventor of the frameless parachute. In 1797 he became the first person to parachute from a balloon. Parachuting at that time involved releasing the hydrogen balloon and descending under a parachute, basket and all. The stunt was first conducted over the Parisian *Parc Monseau*, for which he was made "The Official Aeronaut of France".

Not realizing, or perhaps just not acknowledging, the flight of Elisabeth Thible, Garnerin announced that bringing a woman along on a flight would be his greatest stunt yet. In fact his plans were nearly scuttled by the morals of the time, as people feared that a man and woman alone in a balloon might result in scandalous conduct. In the end, Garnerin convinced the local authorities that the flight would be no more immoral than a mixed couple sharing a carriage.

The woman in question, called *Citoyenne* (Citizen) *Henri*, accompanied Garnerin on a fairly uneventful ascent on June 4, 1798. Like Elisabeth Thible, after her flight nothing else about her seems to have been recorded.

While we have little past, or later, information on Mmes. Thible or Henri, this is not the case for two other notable female aeronauts.

Andres-Jacque Garnerin's wife and pupil, Jeanne-Genevieve, made news on November 10, 1798 by becoming the first woman to pilot a balloon solo. Mme. Garnerin was born Jeanne-Genevieve Labrosse in Paris in 1775. In October, 1797 she watched her future husband make a hydrogen balloon ascent and a parachute descent, his first. They became acquainted and she flew with him 11 months later.

As noted above, a parachute descent from a balloon involved cutting loose the balloon itself and then the occupant rode down in the passenger basket beneath the canopy. In 1802, Jeanne-Genevieve is the person who filed the initial patents for the device, which looks very much as a modern canopy-type parachute might today.

A year after Jeanne-Genevieve met her husband, she made a parachute drop from about 3,000 feet. She and her husband performed throughout Europe and the United Kingdom. Soon Garnerin's niece Elisa would become a part of the act.

Beginning in 1789 the French proletariat revolted against the monarchy, overthrowing King Louis and famously executing both him and Marie Antonette. Napoleon Bonaparte rose to power as a dictator and by 1803 had become embroiled in conflicts with Great Britain. In 1802, before the conflict, however, the Garnerins took their flying show to London. There André made several ascents and parachute descents and, beginning with the third flight, Jeanne accompanied him.

When war broke out in 1803 the Garnerins returned to France where they continued to make flights. In 1806, André-Jacques' niece, Elisa, joined him and Jeanne-Genevieve when she was 15 years old. She is credited with making at least 39 flights with parachute descents before her uncle died in 1823 in an accident while building a balloon.

Jeanne-Genevieve Garnerin lived until 1847 and was a celebrity all of her life. She has a street in *Wissous* named after her.

As famous as Jeanne-Genevieve Garnerin was, however, she was soon overshadowed by another woman aeronaut, Madelaine-Sophie Armant Blanchard.

Jean-Pierre Blanchard made his first hydrogen balloon ascent in March of 1784. He was credited as being the first professional balloonist. Over the course of the next ten years he spent time in England, and toured Europe and the United States demonstrating his ballooning prowess. In January, 1785, he successfully crossed the English Channel from Britain to France, accompanied by an American, Dr. John Jeffries, who had participated in a previous flight from London to Kent.

Blanchard attempted to devise propulsion systems for his balloons that included flapping wings and windmills, but had little success. He did engage in parachuting like Garnerin, and moved from a rigid frame to a folded silk canopy again in parallel with his predecessor.

Sophie Amant Blanchard

In 1804 Blanchard met the much younger Sophie Amant, and Sophie accompanied him on a balloon ride. Normally shy and quiet, Sophie was said to be excited after the flight, describing it as *"sensation incomparable!"* The couple married and set about conducting aerial demonstrations that included Sophie as a solo aeronaut. In 1809, Jeanne-Pierre suffered a heart attack while flying, fell from his balloon, and died from his injuries about a year later.

The tiny Sophie, described as "birdlike" continued to tour and conduct shows. Her balloon gondola was small, silver, and shaped like a decorative boat or cradle. Barely three feet long and with sides only a foot, or so, tall, she stood holding the ropes securing the balloon allowing nearly all of her to be seen. Resplendent in a white Empire style dress, and wearing a feathered hat, she must have been quite the attraction, flying solo and untethered to the ground.

Sophie was known for her night flying, often involving pyrotechnics. She performed for the wedding of Napoleon and Marie-Louise, in 1810, setting off fireworks to celebrate. Later, she flew over Paris dropping leaflets to announce the birth of Napoleon's child. Napoleon made her the *Aéronaute des Fêtes Officielles*, or the Official Aeronaut of Celebrations for France.

After her husband's death, Sophie visited several other cities in Italy, Germany and the United Kingdom. She was known for her exploits and was considered by some as fairly reckless. It is recorded that she became unconscious when she ascended to avoid a hailstorm, and was known to fall asleep in the balloon for hours at a time. While not recorded as such, it would seem that another record might fall to Sophie Blanchard as she was probably the first person to suffer altitude-induced hypoxia, explaining her symptoms.

When Napoleon's dictatorship ended in his ouster in 1814, Sophie quickly switched her allegiance to the restored monarchy. The Bourbon dynasty comprised of the brothers of Louis XVI formed a constitutional monarchy, embracing many of the democratic reforms that came out of the French Revolution. Among her more notable exploits was a balloon flight over the Alps in celebration of Louis XVII birthday. The flight resulted in her suffering nosebleeds and frostbite.

Her nighttime displays got more and more complicated and expansive. It is a shame that there was no way to record in real time the awe-inspiring fireworks shows. She used a complex system of fuses and tapers, setting off glittering cascades and rockets, blue flares known as Bengal lights, as well as suspended static displays. All the while, Sophie, with her brightly colored headdress and white gown stood in her silver gondola illuminated by the bursts, cascades and flares that she carefully choreographed.

The Bourbon government declared her to the "The Official Aeronaut of the Restoration". This was a title for her, only, and not shared with any of her male counterparts, making her, truly, a ground breaking figure in aviation.

It turns out that Sophie Blanchard's quest for more and better spectacle was her undoing. On July 6, 1819 her hydrogen-filled balloon ignited while performing over Paris' Tivoli Gardens. Blanchard fell to the ground and died.

With her death, the mania for ballooning subsided, but women continued to fly in lighter-than-air craft throughout the 19th century. In Germany, Wilhelmine Reichard flew with her chemist and physicist husband, Johann in 1811. The pair, rather than perform stunts, carried out scientific observations. Her first solo flight came the same year and covered over 20 miles at altitudes reaching 16,000 feet. Wilhelmine continued with solo flights throughout the decade. In many cases they were made in order to raise funds for her husband's nascent chemical factory.

Other female balloonists continued to pioneer aviation in Europe, the United Kingdom, Oceania, and the United States. In America, Lizzie Ihling made hot air balloon ascensions in 1876. Her uncle, John Wise was a balloonist of some note in what had become a very competitive field for public appearances at events such as state fairs. Balloon ascents were an effective way to draw a crowd, and Wise, employing his niece, Lizzie, and his grandson and namesake, all flew separate balloons at the same time. To quote an article covering the event from the *Pennsylvania Democratic Watchman*;

> *A balloon ascension at any time is attractive, but when made by a beautiful and accomplished young lady it becomes fascinating – at least to the young men, while the young ladies will be compelled, in sheer self-defense, to turn out en masse, in order to prevent their "gentlemen friends" from becoming too enthusiastic in their admiration of the gay young aeronaut.*

It appears that Ihling's two ascensions were a roaring success, by those terms.

Mary Myers billed herself as "Carlotta, the Lady Aeronaut". Her husband's name was Carl, suggesting that her stage name was meant to fit the package the two created to promote their aeronautical activities. She flew first in 1880 and, by the time she retired in 1891, had made more flights in balloons than anyone else, male or female, in America. She is credited with setting an altitude record of 20,000 feet (accidently), and in developing methods for measuring wind speed, direction and barometric readings that allowed her plot her route of travel by varying altitude.

Susan Adeline Stuart, took the stage name Leona d'Are and performed as a trapeze artist suspended from an ascending balloon in the 1870's. In New Zealand in the 1890's a balloonist named Leila Adair, billed as "The Aerial Queen", also rose seated on a trapeze, performed stunts and ultimately parachuted back to the ground.

Other names and descriptions of female aeronauts, both solo and accompanied, arise in the literature. By the end of the 19th century the use of lighter-than-air craft had taken several turns. As previously shown, balloons, and daredevil acts performed beneath them, became the fodder of circus- and fair-goers. The craft were used for scientific study of meteorology and geography, and militaries had adopted the balloon as an observation platform high above the battlefield, allowing views impossible from ground-based vantages.

Controllable lighter-than-aircraft began to be explored as early as 1852, using steam power. Henri Gifford is credited with building and flying the first steerable ("dirigible") airship in 1852. Also in France, two French Army officers successfully flew an aircraft that was able to return and land where it took off, a major accomplishment given that navigation of airships prior to that depended entirely on the prevailing wind.

Around the turn of the century, inventors like Count Ferdinand von Zeppelin were building airships with rigid frames with the hydrogen lifting gas contained internally in "ballonettes". Zeppelin's LZ-1 (for *Luftschiff Zeppelin*) flew in 1900, becoming the first of a series of ever more advanced aircraft, resulting in Atlantic Ocean crossing luxury liners built by Germany and Great Britain, including the infamous LZ-129 "Hindenburg".

In France, Alberto Santos-Dumont, a Brazilian living in Paris, was pivotal in the development of aviation. Santos-Dumont would go on to build his own airplanes, but, at the time that Zeppelin was beginning to build dirigibles in Germany, Santos-Dumont was building his own in France.

Aida da Costa in 1903

In 1903, the first woman to fly solo in any type of powered aircraft did so in a dirigible. Aida de Acosta, a nineteen-year-old New York socialite, travelled to Paris with her mother, where she got her first look at an airship. Apparently taken by the idea of flying, she took lessons from none other than Santos-Dumont. Santos-Dumont regularly flew his own dirigible, apparently using it as one would a limousine, flying to his favorite restaurant and parking it on the street while he dined. Aida de Costa learned to fly by doing, while Santos-Dumont rode his bicycle alongside giving her instructions. After three lessons, she flew the dirigible to a polo match outside Paris where she, accompanied by Santos-Dumont, watched for a time, and then she flew it back to where she started. This was in June of 1903, more than six months before the Wright Brothers first flight in North Carolina.

As the times would dictate, her parents were scandalized by her actions, her mother telling her that no man would want her for his wife if she acted like that. For another 27 years they tried to hush up the story. In 1930 she recounted the experience to her then husband and a young naval officer over dinner. It is said that Santos-Dumont kept a picture of Aida next to a vase of fresh flowers for the rest of his life, although the two never stayed in touch after the flights.

Aida went on to be twice married. Having lost the sight in one eye to glaucoma, she organized a fund-raising campaign resulting in the establishment of the Wilmer Eye Institute at Johns Hopkins University to honor the surgeon who treated her and saved the sight in her other eye. She became the executive director of the first eye bank in the United States.

As with much to do with aviation and engineering in general, 105 years would elapse before another woman would command a rigid airship.

Throughout the beginning of the 20th century lighter-than-aircraft became an aviation staple. They were used militarily in World War I. After the war Germany was forced to give up its airships but, in 1920's America, three Zeppelin designed dirigibles were built in Lakehurst, New Jersey. After the United States purchased the German-built USS Los Angeles (1923-1924), the larger Macon, Akron and Shenandoah dirigibles were commissioned and launched. The Macon and the Akron were the largest ever built, and each carried five Sparrowhawk fighter planes that could be stored, launched, and recovered making the airships literal flying aircraft carriers.

The Zeppelin LZ-129 "Hindenburg", was 803 feet 10 inches long, and had a volume of 7.1 million cubic feet. The age of the large dirigible ended with the Hindenburg tragedy at Lakehurst in 1937, and was precipitated by the U.S. Navy's loss of all of its airships to weather and crashes between 1925 and 1935. That was not the end of the powered airship, however. The Goodyear Tire and Rubber Company began producing rubber-infused fabric in 1910 and produced their own lighter-than-air (LTA) craft in 1912. Five years later the first "B"-type aircraft, the first "blimp", was built in Chicago and Goodyear established its first LTA base in Akron, Ohio. The U.S. Navy took over and operated the Wingfoot Lake, Ohio facility as its first LTA training base as Goodyear produced both powered and unpowered aircraft and trained Navy personnel.

During the Roaring '20's Goodyear LTA's were used all over the country for exhibitions, much as the balloon had been used a century earlier. The big airships got tagged with the name "Blimp", purportedly because, when deflated, it was just a Type B "limp bag". In 1930 the first blimp carrying the trademark illuminated "Goodyear" sign was launched, a tradition carried on to this day.

When the United States was dragged into the conflict that would become World War II, several blimps were transferred to the U.S. Navy for maritime patrol. With their exceptional ability to remain aloft and loiter for long periods of time, they were very effective in spotting submarines and preventing attacks on shipping in both the Atlantic and Pacific Oceans.

After the war, blimps returned to operation as flying advertisements, and evolved to the uses we see today as camera platforms for sporting events and aerial photography, among other things.

As nearly as can be determined, while airships became more advanced and capable, few female pilots were included in this development since Aida de Acosta took her surreptitious solo flight in France in 1903. And none had flown a rigid airship. A century later that barrier has been broken.

In California in 2008 a startup company called Airship Ventures began flying a thoroughly modern type of Zeppelin airship, offering tours of the San Francisco Bay area. At the controls of the Zeppelin NT (*Neue Technologie*) was Katherine Board. Board was the first female dirigible pilot since 1903

Board is a certificated commercial pilot who thought that flying airliners would be "a bit boring". She was employed by Virgin Lightships, a company providing advertising blimps for flights over events highlighting a company's logo and name, as Goodyear had done for decades. The blimps, built by the American Blimp Corporation, are capable of being illuminated from the inside and are currently the most popular advertising airships in the world. In 1998, Board was offered the opportunity to fly for the Virgin Lightships Company. When Airship Ventures came to be, Board signed on and became the first female Zeppelin NT pilot in the world.

Airship Ventures ceased operations in 2012. Katherine Board left the company before it folded, and went to work for the Zeppelin Company in Germany. In 2011 Airship Ventures hired a pilot with non-rigid airship experience, Andrea Deyling. Deyling, a holder of an air transport pilot certificate quickly adapted to the Zeppelin and became not only a qualified pilot, but a check pilot, the person who trains and certifies others on the type.

Deyling's interest in flight began with a summer aviation camp, and blossomed in the aviation program at Ohio's Kent State University. She flew fixed-wing aircraft before her transition to lighter-than-air, and lists on her *curricula vitae* an around the world trip as a sailor on a tall ship.

With the demise of Airship Ventures, Deyling went to work for Goodyear's airship division. Over the past few years all of the Goodyear blimps have been replaced with rigid craft built on the New Technology platform.

Kristen Arambula, a Chicago resident took per pilot training and became a certified flight instructor at an airport that happened to be the one that blimps used for training when in that area. She managed to get a job with the company whose blimps used that airport when she was just out of college. A couple years of LTA experience later, she contacted Goodyear and got hired to fly for them.

Taylor Laverty Deen was flying as a bush pilot in Alaska. An Oregon native, she moved to San Diego, California in her teens. On vacation abroad with her parents she contemplated the freedom and adventure that could come from being a pilot. After completing her private and commercial ratings in San Diego, and her instructor certifications in Santa Monica, she landed her "bucket list job". She moved to Juneau, Alaska and began flying for a company called Air Excursions. That put her in a situation to traverse some of the most scenic territory in the world, while learning to deal with some of the toughest conditions.

Six months in Alaska, and her contract was expiring. She applied to, and was hired by, Goodyear. Today, she is a Senior Pilot flying Wingfoot II, Goodyear's second *Neue Technologie* airship.

All told, there are four female LTA pilots active at this time. To put that in perspective, they are a small sorority. Much smaller than, say, the number of female astronauts.

CHAPTER 2 - PURPLE POP, POWDER PUFFS, AND ENDURING MYSTERY

Elise Raymonde Deroche was born in Paris in 1882. As a child she had a propensity for sports, and as she grew up, developed an interest in things mechanical, including motorcycles and automobiles. As an actress, she used the stage name Raymonde de Laroche and her place in the aviation pantheon is secured under her *nom de scène*. In 1908 Wilbur Wright, anxious to interest buyers in his family's new technology held demonstration flights in Paris, and de Laroche was witness to his exhibitions.

Raymonde De Laroche

De Laroche was already acquainted with early aviators Ferdinand Léon Delagrange and Charles Voisin, and she went to the Voisin Brothers operations base in order to learn to fly. There are romantic tales of her taxiing in Voisin's single seat biplane while he shouted instructions and then she simply took off and flew at ten or fifteen feet off the ground for about 300 yards with complete control. In reality, she seems to have had extensive teaching from one of the Voisin flight instructors. Either way, she became the first woman to fly a powered, heavier-than-air craft under solo control.

On March 8, 1910, de Laroche became the first woman to gain a license to fly granted by the Aero Club of France, *Fédération Aéronautique Internationale* (FAI), license #36. Always the self-promoter, she began calling herself "Baroness de Laroche", a title that stuck with her during her flying career.

De Laroche participated in numerous "air meetings" in far flung locales including Egypt and Russia. At one of these she suffered a crash that nearly ended her flying career and her life, but after a two year recovery she resumed aviating. In 1913 she was awarded the *Femina Cup* along with 2000 Francs presented by the French *Femina Magazine*. Her accomplishment was a long distance flight of over four hours duration in the air.

When World War I interrupted her flying, she served as a military driver, chauffeuring officers between the rear zones and the front lines, often under fire. After The Great War she returned to flying, setting records for female pilots reaching an altitude of 15,700 feet, traveling a distance 201 miles.

Her aspirations to be a test pilot came to tragedy when, on July 18, 1919, she and a copilot in an experimental airplane crashed on a landing approach and were both killed.

What de Laroche established was a template for many female aviators to follow. France became the training ground for several pioneering woman pilots.

The first American woman to fly solo was Blanche Stuart Scott who was born in New York in 1884. As a young girl she was athletic and daring, becoming an accomplished ice skater and performed tricks while riding her bicycle. Her well-to-do father bought an automobile, a one-cylinder Cadillac and, at age 13, young Blanche began driving the car around Rochester. The city council looked for a way to stop her, but in those days there were no legal restrictions on drivers or vehicles and the concept of a driver's license was still years away.

Blanche Scott's parents were concerned about her rough and tumble activities and, at some point, sent her to finishing school. After three years her rough edges were smoothed a bit, but not her interests in things mechanical. After reading about the coast-to-coast automobile trip by Percy McGargle in a Willys-Overland auto she wrote to the company and proposed that she should be the first woman to make the trip from east to west. Realizing the publicity that would come with her success, the "Lady Overland" departed New York City for San Francisco on May 16, 1910. Her trip would take her and journalist Gertrude Phillips over 5,993 miles of road, only 220 miles of which was paved. The pair reached San Francisco in sixty-seven days. She arrived to a crowd of thousands, as the Willys-Overland publicity team beat her to the West Coast by taking the train, and arranged the greeting.

Passing through Ohio Scott happened upon an airplane in flight from the Wright Brothers' Dayton flying school, which piqued here curiosity about this new adventure. Scott's record road trip caught the attention of Jerome Fanciulli and Glenn Curtiss. They invited her to take flying lessons and to become part of the Curtiss exhibition team.

Her first lessons involved controlling an airplane on the ground with a limiter placed on the throttle, keeping speed below that which was needed to get airborne. On September 6, 1910, however, either the limiter failed or enough headwind caused the airplane to leave the ground. Scott reached and altitude of about 40 feet before bringing the Curtiss pusher biplane in for a smooth and uneventful landing. With that, Blanch Stuart Scott became the first American woman to fly an airplane solo. Her feat, however, was never recognized by the Aeronautical Society of America, although The Early Birds of Aviation, a group founded in 1928 to honor pioneering aviators, did.

Scott performed with the Curtiss team for the next several years, developing a repertoire of stunts, including flying inverted. She did something she called a "Death Dive", dropping nose down from 4000 feet to pull out within 200 feet of the ground. She continued to fly until, in 1916, she quit citing the public's obsession with airplane crashes, and the fact that she saw no real future for women in aviation as the engineering and mechanic jobs were exclusively filled by men.

A mere ten days after Blanche Scott took her first, unplanned flight, a Mineola, New York, businesswoman, physician and dentist, Dr. Bessica Faith Raiche, made a solo airplane flight. Raiche was an avid automobile enthusiast, a linguist, a painter, a musician and was adept at swimming and shooting. She was described as a "proto-feminist". It was the first women's solo recognized by the Aeronautical Society of America.

Unlike Scott's "accidental" flight. Raiche fully intended to fly an airplane, although she had no prior training in doing so.

It is said that Raiche's interest in aviation was born while she was in Paris to study music and witnessed the Raymonde de Laroche flying.

She and her husband François built the Wright-type airplane in the living room of their home. They used bamboo and silk versus the heavier spruce and canvas favored by the Wright brothers. To save additional weight they used piano wire instead of the heavier iron wire used by the Wrights. In fact, the Raiches went on to build two more airplanes as the French-American Aeroplane Company.

Dr. Raiche, like Blanch Stuart Scott, was never officially licensed as a pilot. That honor would go to Harriet Quimby.

Harriet Quimby, 1911

The National Aviation Hall of Fame described Harriet Quimby as, "a modern woman in a not-so-modern age". Born in 1875 in Michigan, her family moved to San Francisco, California around the turn of the twentieth century. California presented a more relaxed attitude to traditional roles, and the girl who grew up as a tomboy and flirted with acting took a stab at journalism as a staff writer for the *San Francisco Dramatic Review*. She was by all accounts a gifted wordsmith and in 1903 she moved to New York City to write as a freelance and drama critic, most notably for *Leslie's Illustrated Weekly*. In 1905 she accepted a full time position with the magazine.

In 1906 Quimby wrote a piece describing her excitement of having ridden in a race car at over 100 miles per hour. She was enraptured with the speed and freedom that automobiles had to offer. This fascination with mechanical things led her to her relationship with the air.

She wrote a piece covering a Japanese aeronaut which led to her spending considerable time at airfields in the New York area. She covered the first American "aviation meeting" held in Los Angeles, and then took an assignment to cover the Belmont Air Meet in New York. This was full on air race, won by an American of Canadian descent, John Moisant, just sneaking by the favorite, Count de Lesseps, a French pilot, at the finish.

Quimby struck up a friendship with Moisant, and convinced *Leslie's* to pay for her flying lessons in exchange for her writing about the experience. Even after Moisant died Quimby continued her quest, producing articles that not only described how women should dress when aviating, but describing the technical aspects of aircraft mechanics and control. She followed the exploits of male aviators like Glenn Curtiss and Lincoln Beachy who were setting records and drawing crowds. When she started getting fan mail addressed to "The Bird Girl" she was committed to seeing her pilot education through.

On August 1, 1911, Quimby was issued FAI License #37, administered by the Aero Club of America, becoming the first woman to earn a pilot certificate in the United States. Then she set about building her persona as an aviator. As wearing a dress and aviating were incompatible, she had made for herself a flying suit of violet satin, which only served to make her more photogenic and in demand.

In 1910, pioneering aviator Calbraith Perry "Cal" Rogers obtained sponsorship for a coast-to-coast flight from the Armour Meat Packing Co. who had begun to sell a grape soda called "Vin Fiz". The Vin Fiz name was painted prominently on the wings of his Wright biplane, becoming what has to be the earliest aviation product tie-in ever. In 1912, the Vin Fiz crashed off the coast of Long Beach, California, and Rogers was killed.

Needing a spokesperson, the aviator-journalist in the grape colored flying suit was a match perfectly made. With Vin Fiz sponsorship, Quimby promoted the product in her flying and, in turn, graced advertisements for the product throughout her career. Without these print ads we would likely not be able to see Quimby and her flying togs in full color.

Quimby joined an exhibition group that included her friend John's widow, Matilde Moisant. Flying with this group became a way to make money, and she collected $700 for performing the first ever night flight by a woman. She is credited with making the checklist an integral part of flying and for drawing attention that brought many others into aviation, including men. "If a woman can do it, so can I".

On July 25, 1909, aviator and airplane constructor Louis Blériot took off from the coast of France and, flying over open water, collected a £1000 prize put up by the London Daily Mail for the first successful flight across the English Channel. Quimby's flying career reached its zenith when on April 16, 1912, she duplicated Bleriot's feat, in a similar Beriot XI monoplane.

On July 12, 1912, Quimby was flying a new Bleriot XI-2 two place monoplane from Boston over the harbor and around the Boston Light, returning to land. Circling the field and back out over the water, at about 1000 feet the airplane pitched forward in a near vertical dive and both Quimby and her passenger were ejected and both died at the scene.

Harriet Quimby did, however, establish the benchmarks and the path that female aviators would follow for years to come.

Ruth Bancroft Law was born in Massachusetts in 1887. Her brother, Rodman was two years older, and both children were physically fit and active. Rodman was stunt man, and Ruth challenged herself to be as good as he was at everything. She wanted to learn to fly, and approached the great Orville Wright for lessons, only to be turned down. He apparently believed that women were not mechanically inclined and, therefore, incapable of learning to fly. Of course, Law's attitude was, "The surest way to make me do a thing is to tell me I can't do it."

She took flying lessons from Massachusetts aviators Harry Atwood and Arch Freeman, and earned her pilot license in 1912. By 1915 she was performing aerobatics in a Curtiss pusher biplane, and performed s double loop, much to the chagrin of her now husband, Charles Oliver.

Ruth Bancroft Law

She attempted to set altitude records in competition in 1916, narrowly missing a win to a male aviator. With that, she decided she would go after a distance record. She set her sights on Chicago to New York, non-stop.

Somewhat incredulously, the Aero Club of America agreed to sanction her attempt. Her 100 horsepower Curtiss required the pilot to have both hands on controls at all times, so she devised a method of navigating that included her course notes written on the cuffs of her flying gloves, and her maps on a roller device strapped to her seatbelt and seat arm rest. She could use her right knee for short periods to control the plane while she turned the maps.

The Curtiss offered no protection from the elements as the pilot sat on a perch ahead of the wing. Many felt that a woman would not be able to endure the rigors of the flight of some 590 non-stop miles.

The plane only had a 16-gallon fuel tank, so Law added on to up the capacity to 53 gallons.

After a dicey take off in stiff and gusty winds that forced her to fly below 200 feet, she finally got things sorted much to the relief of the onlookers watching her departure. Hour after hour, reports came in from towns on her route: Vermillion, Ohio, then McKean, Pennsylvania. This meant she was on track and had a good chance of success. Headwinds finally found her out of fuel a couple of miles from Hormell, New York, her objective. She managed to glide the last bit and landed to the thrill of supporters and onlookers. She had averaged 103 miles per hour for 590 miles, smashing the existing distance record for female aviators by nearly 150 miles.

After refueling, and a bite to eat the local hotel, she departed for New York City. Her take off from Hormel was almost thwarted by tall trees around the field, once again causing fear amongst the gathered spectators that the flight was going to come to a bad end. Law described branches scraping the bottom of the airplane as she climbed out.

The second leg ended in Binghampton, as dark fell and she couldn't continue. She flew on to New York City the next morning, and had to pick her way up the Susquehanna River to the Delaware River, then over a range of hills to the Hudson, through fog to finally reach Governor's Island, her destination.

With that, she set the record for the longest distance flown by any American, male or female. She broke a record set by Victor Carlstrom who flew a much more modern, 200 horsepower Curtiss with a 200 gallon fuel capacity. And, she became a national hero.

Ruth Law Oliver, at the urging of her husband, quit flying in 1922, but only after setting more records for distance and altitude, and encouraging young people to take up flying, no matter their gender.

Katherine Stinson was born in Alabama in 1891, and raised in Mississippi. A biographical children's book describes Katherine and her sister, Marjorie "flying" on a swing as little girls in Canton. She apparently solidified her desire to fly when she had the opportunity to ride in a hot air balloon, and she and her mother began collecting information on the inventive Wright brothers and their new flying machine. Her intentions gained solidity when, with her mother, they watched an exhibition flight of the Wright Flyer. She had dreams of becoming a concert pianist, and had a piano that she had won in a contest. Somehow, she determined that she could pay for her music studies by learning to fly and performing air shows for money, so, in 1911, she sold her piano to pay for flying lessons. A contemporary news article said that "barnstorming pilots or exhibition pilots were earning $1,000 dollars a show."

She traveled to St. Louis, Missouri in order to take flying lessons from Tony Jannus, who had made a name for himself as an exhibition and stunt pilot. It appears that Jannus took Katherine on one or more rides in his airplane, but would not let her fly. In St. Louis, she got the same treatment from a Wright pilot, Max Lillie, who told her that she was, at five feet tall, and barely one hundred pounds, too small and light to be a pilot. She is said to have told Lillie that flying was about physical and mental coordination, which was not a matter of physical size or strength.

In the end, Lillie relented and gave her lessons. The Wright Flyer used two hand operated sticks to control the plane, so her first lessons were on a simulator built of sawhorses and wood. Actual flight instruction involved Lillie sitting on the lower wing next to Katherine while she flew the airplane. She was able to solo a Wright Flyer after four hours of instruction. At barely twenty-one years old, she became the fourth American woman ever to earn her FAI flying license.

Katherine, with her diminutive size and youthful visage came to be called "The Flying Schoolgirl".

Katherine's sister Marjorie was four years younger. She followed her big sister's lead into the air by attending the Wright flying school in Dayton, Ohio. She gained her pilot's license in August, 1914 and was the ninth American women to do so. At age eighteen, she was, also, the youngest woman flyer in the country.

Katherine, Eddie and Marjorie Stinson

The sisters, along with their brother Eddie, moved to San Antonio, Texas in 1915. They managed to convince the city that a flying school would be of value, and leased five hundred acres a few miles south of downtown, just west of the San Antonio River. The rent was to be five dollars per year.

The Stinsons taught civilians to fly, as well as students from the Royal Canadian Air Force. World War I brought civilian flight training to a halt, but the field survived in the hands of the city of San Antonio, and remains today as Stinson Field (KSSF), a general aviation airport.

The sisters were notable for a number of other aviation firsts and feats.

In 1913, Katherine and her mother, Emma, living in Arkansas, founded the Stinson Aviation Company. This resulted in her making what is surely the first air mail flights performed by a female pilot. It also gave her a base of operations to pursue her ambitions as a performer. Katherine, "The Flying Schoolgirl" toured the country, becoming an exhibition flyer.

She flew a Curtiss JN-4 "Jenny" during her career, as well as a specially modified JN model equipped with a radial engine called a Curtiss-Stinson "Special". The radial engine used in this customized aircraft previously belonged to Lincoln Beachy, the pioneering exhibition aviator, and was acquired after he died in a crash.

In 1915, she became the first woman to perform a loop in an airplane, and later added a roll to the maneuver, thrilling the crowds. At an exhibition in Pasadena, California, she flew a pattern while training smoke that spelled out "C A L", becoming the first female skywriter.

Katherine went on to set several long distance records, many in Canada, and a non-stop flight from San Diego to San Francisco, California, just shy of 400 miles. When the United States entered World War I and the flying school closed, Katherine traded her aviating for humanitarian service, becoming an ambulance driver with the Red Cross in Europe. She wanted to become a pilot for the U.S. Army Air Corps when the country entered the war in Europe, but was rejected because of her gender. This, in spite of the fact that she was demonstrably a better pilot than most of the men sent to the front.

Returning to the U.S. post-war, in 1918 she is credited for a non-stop flight from Chicago, Illinois to Binghamton, New York, a flight of about 520 miles.

Katherine contracted influenza in Europe that resulted in lung damage and a susceptibility to tuberculosis and ended her flying career.

While Katherine was "The Flying Schoolgirl", her sister Marjorie became known as "The Flying Schoolmarm". This was the result of her having taught over one hundred students at the family flight school in San Antonio. As many of these were Royal Canadian Air Force (RCAF) pilots, her group became known as "The Texas Escadrille".

In August, 1914, an event called a Suffrage Field Day was held in Chicago. Marjorie and Katherine flew a Wright biplane towing a yellow "Votes for Women" banner over the event. Marjorie became very active in the Women's suffrage movement and used her flying to raise funds for the effort. Her patriotic efforts weren't limited to getting the vote. She campaigned after the war for a Victory Memorial in Washington, D.C., and tied flights to selling Victory Bonds.

In 1915, Marjorie became the only woman pilot admitted into the U.S. Aviation Reserve Corps, and the only woman granted a license through the Army and Navy Committee of Aeronautics.

Katherine Stinson married a prominent New Mexico politician and jurist and spent her later years as an architect in Santa Fe. She died at age 86, in 1977.

Marjorie Stinson continued to fly and was a charter member of the Ninety-Nines. She worked as a draftsperson for the Aeronautical Division of the U.S. Navy, retiring in 1945. She passed away in 1976, and her ashes were spread from an airplane over Stinson Field in San Antonio.

Phoebe Omlie was born Phoebe Jane Fairgrave in Des Moines, Iowa in 1902. She moved with her family to St. Paul Minnesota when she was 12, and finished high school there. The day before her graduation President Woodrow Wilson visited Minneapolis and was honored with a flyover which she witnessed and became intrigued with flying.

She began hanging out at an airfield near her home, trying to convince the manager to let one of his flight instructors take her flying. Having had enough, he agreed to take her up with the intent of scaring the desire to fly out of her by performing aerobatic maneuvers. Rather than getting air sick or frightened, she demanded more flight time and, using some inheritance money, bought herself a Curtiss JN-4 "Jenny" biplane.

Fairgrave let other pilots fly her plane while she learned an increasingly daring repertoire of aerial tricks. These included barnstormer's staples like wing walking, hanging from the plane by a strap in her teeth, and performing the Charleston on the top wing of the airplane. She learned to parachute and set a women's record jumping from 15,200 feet. All of this garnered her and her pilot, Vernon Omlie, a movie deal and flying scenes in the popular movie serial, "The Perils of Pauline". The pair toured the country barnstorming and in 1922 married.

In 1925 the pair moved to Memphis, Tennessee and opened a flight school. In 1927 she became the first female licensed airplane mechanic and received her air transport pilot license, another first for a woman.

Working for the Mono Aircraft Company in 1928, Phoebe Omlie set an altitude record for female pilots flying a Monocoupe 90 to 25,400 feet. Later that same year she competed in the Ford Reliability Tour, becoming the first woman to cross the Rocky Mountains as the pilot of an airplane.

During the 1920's air racing and record setting were the *raison d'etre* for much of aviation. Major companies and publication put up money prizes for a number of "firsts", leading to feats such as Charles Lindbergh's epic flight across the Atlantic to Paris in the Ryan monoplane "Spirit of St. Louis". Female aviators became well established as barnstormers and competitors, but often, were relegated to separate events.

In 1929, as part of the National Air Races and Aeronautical Exposition, the event organizer, Cliff Henderson established the first "Women's Air Derby". Like many events held for male aviators, it was a cross-country event to be held over several days, flying from Santa Monica, California to Cleveland, Ohio. Planes were divided into "heavy" and "light" classes and pilots had to have at least 100 hours of logged flying time, 25 hours of which was cross-country, just like the male pilots. There was a qualification that the airplane had to have "horsepower appropriate for a woman", which led one competitor to seek an alternative aircraft when her 300 horsepower Travel Air was disallowed.

The list of competitors reads like a Who's Who of female aviation pioneers and personalities. Along with Pheobe Omlie flying a "light class" plane, she would be in the air with the likes of Louise Thaden, Bobbi Trout, Ruth Elder, Florence "Pancho" Barnes, and Amelia Earhart.

The famed humorist, friend of Wylie Post, and aviation enthusiast Will Rogers called this race the "Powderpuff Derby".

With 18,000 people on hand in Cleveland to witness the finish of the race, Louise Thadden won the "heavy class" with a time of 20 hours and 19 minutes. Pheobe Omlie won the "Light Class" in 25 hours and 12 minutes.

Omlie went on to hold several positions with the federal government, including Special Advisor for Air Intelligence for the National Advisory Committee for Aeronautics (NACA), and worked beside Amelia Earhart in helping to build what would become the National Air Space System, familiar to all pilots today. She would be involved in the creation of the Civilian Pilot Training Program at 66 airports nationwide that would include CPTP schools at Chicago's Harlem Airport and in Tuskegee, Alabama, which resulted in the Tuskegee Airmen.

In November, 1929, after the inaugural Women's Air Derby, Amelia Earhart called for a meeting of all of the licensed female pilots in the U.S. at Curtiss Field in Valley Stream, New York. The initial group of twenty-six women met upstairs in a hangar and established that, "Membership would be open to any woman with a pilot's license, and the purpose was 'good fellowship, jobs, and a central office and files on women in aviation'".

The Ninety-Nines inaugural meeting

35

After much discussion about what to call themselves (suggestions included "Noisy Birdwomen", "Homing Pigeons", and "Gadflies") it was determined that the number of charter members would be used. Over the period of organization, this number climbed from eighty-six, to ninety-seven and, finally became "The Ninety Nines". At the time, there was a total one hundred twenty seven licensed female pilots

The roster of charter members contains some of the greatest influencers in aviation. Louise Thaden, for instance, in 1929 held world records for speed, endurance and altitude in light planes, and went on to win the Women's Air Derby of 1929 outright. In 1936, female aviators succeeded in pressuring the organizers of the world famous Bendix Trophy Air Race to allow women to compete. Thaden partnered with Blanche Noyes, also a charter member of the Ninety-Nines, to fly a Beech C-17R "Staggerwing" biplane from New York to Los Angeles, beating several male pilots, many in purpose-built racing planes.

Evelyn "Bobbi" Trout, so called because she adopted a "bob" hairstyle, first flew at sixteen years old, and proceeded to make her living in aviation. She is most noted for holding several endurance records, including an all-night flight, remaining aloft for over seventeen hours in an open cockpit biplane. Her final record saw her and co-pilot Edna Mae Cooper fly for 122 hours 50 minutes, earning her a record, and a royal decree and Aviation Cross bestowed by the King of Romania. The only other recipients of this award are Amelia Earhart and Charles Lindbergh.

Arguably the most famous Ninety-Nine of all was Amelia Earhart. The Earhart sisters, Amelia and Grace, "Meeley" and "Pidge", were by all accounts, "active" children. Their mother apparently gave them considerable leeway in both behavior and dress which allowed the girls to engage in "rough and tumble" activities, including having an extensive collection of bugs, and the creation of a makeshift roller coaster using the roof of the tool shed, a cobbled up ramp, and a wooden box. The inaugural run resulted in a bruised lip, a torn dress, and Meeley's comment, "Oh, Pidge, it's just like flying!"

Earhart's first encounter with a flying machine did little to get her interested, apparently. At age 10, she saw her first plane at the Iowa State Fair and her father offered to pay for rides for the two sisters. Earhart is said to have wanted to go back to the merry-go-round, as to her eye, the plane looked rickety and unsafe.

Several sources report that Earhart was always interested in a career in science, technology, law or film directing, choices not thought to be appropriate for girls in the 1910's. She made several stabs at classes in high school and junior college but failed to follow through. With the World War raging in 1917 she volunteered as a nurse's aide in Toronto, Ontario, working with wounded veterans, a job that continued into 1918 as Spanish Flu rocked that city.

She had her next encounter with an airplane at the Canadian National Exhibition when a veteran fighter pilot decided to "buzz" her and her friend who were standing in a clearing. "I did not understand it at the time," she said, "but I believe that little red airplane said something to me as it swished by."

In 1920, Earhart finally took an airplane ride, and that ten-minute flight apparently cemented her ambitions. By early 1922 she had completed flying lessons in Long Beach, California, bought herself a leather flying jacket and cropped her hair in the style of other female aviators. Later that year she bought a yellow Kinner Airster biplane that she called "the Canary" which she flew in October to her first record for female pilots, an altitude of 14,000 feet.

In May, 1923 she obtained her FAI pilot certificate, #6017, and became the sixteenth American woman to hold an FAI license.

The details of her personal and professional life that followed are richly recorded in virtually dozens of books, articles, and video presentations. Germane to this chapter are Earhart's aviation accomplishments, and her one most notable failure.

In 1928 Earhart flew as a passenger and log keeper on a twenty-plus hour flight from Newfoundland to Wales in a Fokker Trimotor piloted by Wilmer Stultz and his copilot and mechanic, Louis Gordon, making her the first woman transatlantic passenger. This piqued her desire to be the first female pilot to accomplish this feat. Stultz flew the bulk of the time on instruments, something that Earhart was not yet trained to do. None of that stopped her from being a part of the celebration given the trio in England, and again with a ticker tape parade in New York and a presidential reception at the White House.

Her relationship to journalist and publicist George Putman certainly did not hinder her ascension in the press to "Queen of the Air". She received offers for endorsements for lines of women's sportswear, luggage and, even, *Lucky Strike* cigarettes. Her celebrity allowed her a platform to promote aviation, working at times alongside the superstar aviator of the period, Charles Lindbergh.

While in England Earhart flew an Avro Avian III airplane that was owned by a British noble, Lady Mary Heath, which she then purchased and had shipped back to the United States. It was in this airplane, as her star was rising rapidly, that she flew solo across North America and back. Male pilots who flew with her generally lauded her skills as a pilot, and in 1929, as noted above, she entered the Women's Air Derby. After a late start necessitated by a return to the field to repair a broken starter motor,

Earhart maintained a fourth place position throughout the race, finishing third when the third place competitor, Ruth Nichols, drifted into construction equipment when landing and wound up upside down, short of the finish line.

In the early 1930's, Earhart successfully lobbied the *Fédération Aéronautique Internationale* to establish categories for separate women's records, consistent with the policy in the United States. She then proceeded to, in 1931, set an altitude record of 18,415 feet flying an autogyro (an aircraft using an unpowered rotary wing for lift and a propeller for thrust). While many of her exploits appeared to be "stunts", her aim in performing them, as well as her involvement in the National Aeronautic Association and in the Ninety-Nines, was meant to promote an interest in aviation among the general public and, particularly, among women.

Earhart eventually married George Putman which put her even closer to a number of contemporary movers and shakers, to many of whom, by virtue of that relationship, she was now related. She owned a red Lockheed Vega monoplane that would prove central in many of her most daring exploits. The first of these found her becoming the first woman to fly across the Atlantic, departing Grace Harbour, Newfoundland and landing in a pasture north of Derry, Northern Ireland just short of fifteen hours later. This flight garnered her a Congressional Distinguished Flying Cross, the French Legion of honor, and a Gold Medal from the National Geographic Society.

Earhart made friends with influential women, including Eleanor Roosevelt who would become First Lady of the United States in 1933, and who continued to show an interest in, and promote aviation throughout her life. Mrs. Roosevelt was as influential as anyone in ultimately establishing the flight schools at Chicago and Tuskegee that resulted in the famed "Tuskegee Airmen". Another friend made during this period began as her most notable flying rival and eventually the driving force behind the more than one thousand female pilots that during World War II contributed mightily to the war effort, the Women's Airforce Service Pilots. Her name was Jacqueline Cochran.

In 1935, Earhart became the first aviator, male or female, to fly from solo from Hawaii to the mainland, Honolulu to Oakland, California, in her now signature red Vega.

1937 found her living in Southern California with her husband now involved with Paramount Pictures in Hollywood, and she fell under the tutelage of Frank Mantz, the owner of United Air Services and Burbank Airport. Mantz helped her hone her long distance flying skills, and it was fortuitous that the Lockheed Aircraft Company was based at the same field. As plans for a flight circumnavigating the globe emerged, Earhart conceded that her single-engine Vega would not be capable of a journey like that. Her connections through Mantz and, and her ownership of a Lockheed record setting plane, set the stage for the construction of specially modified, twin-engine, twin tail Lockheed Electra 10E airliner.

In March, 1937, her first attempt at a round-the-world flight began in Oakland, California with Mantz as technical advisor, and Harry Manning as copilot, and reversed the route of her solo Pacific flight, landing in Honolulu, Hawaii. Mechanical issues *en route*, and then a problem on takeoff, forced her to abandon the attempt and have the airplane returned to California by ship.

At the end of May, 1937, Earhart flew her Electra from Oakland, California to Miami, Florida on the first, but unpublicized, leg of her next famed round-the-world attempt. Seasonal changes in winds made the west-to-east route more favorable, dictating the change in direction. At Miami she went public with her plans, and on June 1, she took off accompanied by Fred Noonan, an experienced ship's captain, and the person who had established most of the seaplane routes for Pan American Airways, as navigator.

Earhart and Noonan plotted a route that would take them around the broadest part of globe, planning to fly about 29,000 miles in all. From Miami, the pair flew through South America, Africa, South Asia and Australia, landing at Lae, New Guinea on June 29.

What followed remains the fodder for endless speculation. Whether a matter of pilot or navigator error, poor pre-flight decisions surrounding communications equipment, or intriguing hypotheses regarding anti-Japanese espionage, at this writing no definitive explanation of how or where the pair was lost exists. What is known is that the route was supposed to take the ill-fated Electra over nearly twenty six hundred miles of open water to a spot of land one and one quarter miles long and about three eights of a mile wide. Their success hinged entirely on their being able to communicate with, and use the signals from, the U.S. Coast Guard Cutter *Itasca* , for directional reference. Later research would point to issues with incompatible radios and frequencies, both parties using different time references (Greenwich Mean Time vs. Naval Standard Time), and Noonan's inability to use Morse Code as factors.

Amelia Earhart was the preeminent female aviator of her time, but only one of many who spread the gospel of flight to women across America, and worldwide. From the time of Harriet Quimby to Amelia Earhart's era, aviation in America grew exponentially, and American women in aviation grew in lockstep. When war embroiled the United States again, women were ready to step up and make a meaningful difference in the outcome.

CHAPTER 3 –
THE FIRST BLACK FIGHTER PILOT

Eugene J. Bullard 1917

In Georgia. USA, after the Civil War, plantations formerly using slave labor still farmed cotton, while the former slaves became sharecroppers and were now paid for their labors. William Octave Bullard was such a person, having been born in 1863. In 1890, Bullard married a woman of Native American descent and moved 40 miles upriver, from the plantation on which he had always lived, to Columbus, Georgia.

Columbus approaching the turn of the 20th Century, was a typical rural southern town. Much of its commerce involved the processing and shipping of cotton. William Bullard took a job loading bales onto ships, working for a Mr. W.C. Bradley. Bullard was, by all accounts, strong, a hard worker and well-liked by his employer. A big man, at about 6 foot 4 inches, he was given the nickname "Big Chief Ox", reflecting his size, his middle name, and his marriage to a Creek woman

Over twelve years, his family grew to include ten children. The seventh child, Eugene James Bullard was born in 1895. His biography says that he grew up a "very happy child" and loved to play with friends and ride his goat drawn cart around the neighborhood. His mother, however, was careful to keep him from playing with white children, so he was shielded from the racial attitudes of the times. That was, until his mother died when he was seven years old. When he did finally meet white children, they taunted him and called him names.

William Bullard had much the same problem at his job. Despite his good relationship with his employer, Mr. Bradley, his supervisor called Stevens, by all accounts, disliked Black people, and "would curse at them and kick and hit them." One day, he turned his ire on William "Ox" Bullard, who proceeded to ignore him. Stevens became very agitated and angry and hit Bullard in the head with an iron loading hook. To his surprise, Bullard remained standing even though he was bleeding profusely.

Bullard, enraged, picked up the hapless Stevens and threw him headlong down a loading hole in the floor of the warehouse. Mr. Bradley tried to defend Bullard, telling people that Stevens fell through the hole. Even though Stevens survived, Bradley told Bullard to go home, lock the door and hide.

As might be expected in the post-Reconstruction South, a mob soon formed at the warehouse. Drinking and shouting they marched to and converged on the Bullard home and banged on the locked door. Bullard and his family stayed out of sight long enough for the lynch mob to decide that Bullard couldn't possibly be dumb enough to go home, and dispersed.

As children, the Bullards would listen to their father talk about a world where everyone was treated equally, and he told them of a magical place called France were white people were nice and polite to everyone, including Black people. After the incident that forced his father into an extended absence, Eugene decided he would leave home and go to France. Of course, he had no idea where France was, or what direction he needed to go, but he was determined.

Just short of his eleventh birthday, Eugene sold his goat for $1.50, and set out to find France. He spent his first night away in a Travelers camp. What happened over the next few years is enough adventure to fill a book. In fact, there are several, including his memoirs and biographies.

Seeing no chance to get to France with the Romany Travelers, Eugene took off and followed railroad tracks until he met a sharecropper family that took him in for the night. They let him help with chores, and gave him a dollar. The money was just enough for one-way train fare to Atlanta. There, at the stockyards, he met another band of Travelers and learned about the care and training of horses. The Romanys told him that they traveled all over North America and Europe, but, after finding out that they had no intention of going back to Europe for at least a couple of years, Eugene set out again.

On the road, Eugene was offered a ride by a white man named Travis Moreland. Moreland offered Eugene a meal and a place to stay. Moreland told Eugene the next day that he couldn't leave, and began to treat him as if he was a slave. Eugene, upset, confronted Moreland about his cursing and poor treatment, to which Moreland responded by agreeing to no longer call him demeaning names, and to pay him 50 cents a day to work on his place. Eugene worked for six months for Moreland, then set out once again to find France.

Over the next few months, he lived in Sasser, Georgia, working for a barber. Although white, the barber, Mr. Matthews, treated Eugene with kindness. When Eugene got exceedingly ill, spiking a fever of 105 degrees, Matthews called, and paid for a doctor to treat Eugene.

Eugene made it to Dawson City, Georgia where he was hired by a Zacharias Turner to care for his horses and do stable work. Eugene had adopted the name "Gypsy", from the common and demeaning term used for the Romany Travelers, and had used it intermittently since his first encounter the Travelers. Turner traded in horses and mules from Texas. Eugene so impressed Turner with his ability to tend to and train the animals that in 1911 Turner entered him as a jockey at the Terrell County State Fair. Eugene, resplendent in red and yellow silks, was the only jockey of color entered. At about 16 years old, his riding skills brought him a win by a length-and-a-half, making him a hero to the Black community in the area.

Four months later, Eugene packed up the clothes he had been secreting, and the money he had saved. Turner had him deliver a pony to St. Andrews Bay, Florida. Rather than returning to Georgia, he bought a railway ticket to Montgomery, Alabama. Several menial jobs later, Eugene had saved up $16.00, and had made his way to Atlanta.

Still not knowing how to get to France, "where all colored folks are treated right by everybody", Eugene started to ride the rails. He first hopped a train, hiding in the undercarriage of a dining car, bound for Richmond, Virginia. He jumped the train when it stopped near Jamestown, Virginia. Short of his destination, he found work at some odd jobs for a few days while trying to figure out which train would take him to Richmond and, then, the Atlantic coast. As luck would have it, he wound up in Newport News, a major Virginia seaport.

Ever on the lookout for opportunity, Eugene watched men loading cargo on a sailing ship. With no idea of where it was bound, he hoped that getting out to sea meant getting closer to France. He fell in line with the stevedores and was laden with a heavy crate of cabbages to take on board. Once there, he found a hiding place among large cotton bales and settled in for his voyage. A few hours out of Newport News, the ship stopped. Eugene had made it as far as Norfolk, Virginia.

As a major trading port, Norfolk offered more opportunities. Eugene managed to get aboard the *Mart Russ*, a German cargo ship bound for Aberdeen, Scotland, and Hamburg, Germany. He stowed away in a lifeboat until, still nearly three weeks away from its first stop, he ran out of the food and water that he brought aboard.

Hungry and thirsty, he came out of hiding and found the ship's galley. The man he encountered turned out to be the same one who, the night before the ship sailed, had paid Eugene a dime to take a bucket to a local bar and bring him back some beer. Apparently startled to see Eugene again, this German sailor said he had to report Eugene to the captain. He was kind enough, however, to give Eugene food and drink, and advise him on how to deal with the ship's captain.

Captain Westphal threatened to throw Eugene overboard, but, quickly relented and put him to work engine room. For two and a half weeks Eugene hauled ashes up from the ship's boilers and threw them overboard. Upon reaching Aberdeen, Scotland, Captain Westphal paid Eugene $25.00 for his work and Eugene set off to find France.

Eugene kicked around Aberdeen while gaining information on how to get the last few miles between him and France behind him. We worked as a dancer with a hurdy-gurdy man, and then as a lookout for a riverfront gambler. Apparently watching for the police turned out to be both easy and profitable for Eugene. It earned him enough to live on and to purchase train fare to Liverpool, an ideal place from which to sail to France.

In Liverpool, Eugene took a number of odd jobs, including as a stevedore, an assistant on a fish wagon, and working at an amusement park on weekends as a target for a "hit-the-man-with-the rubber-ball" game.

With weekdays free to explore, Eugene found himself at Chris Baldwin's Gymnasium. Baldwin assessed Eugene as having, with proper training, potential as a boxer. At 112 pounds, Eugene would have fought as a bantamweight. Using the money he earned from his other jobs, he spent his off time working out and learning boxing moves.

By the time he turned seventeen, Eugene had bulked up and felt he was ready for a real bout. It was arranged that he take on the Irish boxer, Bill Welsh, in a ten-round professional lightweight fight. On the same card was an African-American boxer called Lister Brown, known professionally as "The Dixie Kid".

Brown fought first, knocking out his English opponent in the second round. When it came Eugene's turn, he traded punches with Welsh for the entire ten rounds. With both men standing at the end of the fight, the decision came on points. The referee held up Eugene's gloved hand as the winner. The Dixie Kid, who had been in the audience, approached Eugene with an offer to come with him to London to train. Eugene accepted.

Over the next couple of years, Eugene fought regularly, and lived in a boarding house that catered to other boxers and entertainers from all over the world. Eugene still wanted to go to France, though. Knowing that, Brown managed to arrange a boxing match for December 3, 1913, against a French fighter, Georges Forrest, in Paris.

One can only imagine the excitement that Eugene must have felt getting his first glimpse of the coast of France while crossing the English Channel. Likewise, one would think that his arrival in Paris must have been more than memorable. Eugene had a few days to take in some of the "City of Lights" before his bout, and a few days after. He won, again on points, the twenty round fight, making him a Parisian sensation.

Back in England, Eugene looked for ways to get back to Paris. With no boxing opportunities on the horizon, he managed to join a minstrel show. He had shown himself to be a born entertainer with his jobs in Scotland, and "Freedman's Pickaninnies" brought him a chance to travel throughout Europe doing real "slapstick" comedy.

Early in 1914, the troupe travelled to Paris. When the "Pickaninnies" left town, they did so without him. By the spring of 1914, Eugene had landed other jobs, learned to speak French, and even changed is middle name to "Jacques". With that, Eugene sought to make France his permanent home.

The next couple of months proved instrumental in Eugene's becoming, as he billed himself later in life, "The World's First Black Fighter Pilot". Over the course of a few days in July, 1914, a Bosnian separatist assassinated the Archduke Ferdinand of Austria and his wife. As the weapon used had come from Serbia, the Austro-Hungarian Empire threatened violence. Allied with the Serbians, both the French and the Russians mobilized troops forming fronts surrounding Germany, an ally of Austria, leading to the onset of a war that dragged in virtually all of Europe and, eventually, The United States.

Eugene Bullard, wanting to serve his adopted France, tried to join the French armed services but, as a non-citizen, was banned from serving in the regular army or navy. He, instead, joined the French Foreign Legion, which accepted enlistees from anywhere.

What ensued was, surely, the bloodiest conflict in history. War was fought from opposing trenches. Under heavy fire from rifles, machine guns, and artillery, soldiers on either side would take any opportunity to climb out and advance across a "no man's land" toward the enemy in hopes of forcing a retreat. This sort of fighting went on day after day, leaving many, or most, of the soldiers on either side dead on the middle ground. With the ferocity of each attack, neither side had the ability to recover their casualties, leaving men where they fell.

On Christmas Day, 1914, a truly astonishing thing occurred. The soldiers from both sides declared a cease-fire. Both opposing armies were able to retrieve their dead comrades and even sang carols and exchanged small gifts. This miracle lasted only until German officers got wind of the situation and one of them picked up a rifle and killed a French soldier. Once more all hell broke loose.

Eugene survived four months of trench warfare near Sommes, France before being relieved for rest behind the lines. His respite was short-lived, however, as his unit was put back into action behind the front lines digging trenches, laying telephone cable, and hauling supplies near Artois. There, it is recorded, that Eugene heard an airplane buzzing overhead, and wondered if he was capable of flying one.

In May, the French launched a full-scale attack on the Germans. Heavily fortified, the Germans fought back. Of the 250 Legionnaires in his unit, only 54 survived. Fighting at times was reduce to hand-to-hand in the trenches. By July, with the Germans driven from the area, Eugene's remaining comrades were ordered out of battle. Not enough men survived to maintain the Third Marching Regiment, so the soldiers were folded into the elite First Regiment of the Legion, and Eugene became Corporal Bullard, receiving a battlefield promotion.

Over the next several months, Bullard fought the Germans in huge, pitched trench battles. Bullard suffered a wound to the head, but, fortunately, the steel helmet had recently replaced the cloth kepi as the battle headgear of the French. In fact, his steel helmet undoubtedly saved his life as an artillery shell sprayed shrapnel, giving him a deep cut on his head, while extensively denting the helmet. At Verdun the Germans unleashed massive artillery attacks decimating the French troops. At one point, so few of his First Legionnaire brothers survived that the unit, all comprised of foreign soldiers, was disbanded and folded into the 170th Infantry Regiment, called by the Germans "The Swallows of Death". Bullard was made a machine gunner. Over the course of three days at the beginning of March, 1916, Bullard survived a poison gas attack, an artillery explosion that sent shrapnel that knocked out his front teeth and, after tending to 11 wounded men from the same shell, made his way back to the command post only to be blown through the front door by another exploding round. Told that he had to fall back for medical treatment, he refused. He and his commander returned to the wounded soldiers left in the farmhouse were Bullard was first injured.

That evening, after getting treatment for his wounds, Bullard returned to the fight, firing belt after belt of machine gun bullets until his gun jammed, a result of debris kicked up by a close artillery hit. Bullard fell back to the rear trenches, but the following night went out with members of his team to scavenge another machine gun, ammunition and food. Taking the fight back to the advancing Germans, another cannon round blew up near enough to Bullard to kill ten members of his unit and leave him with a large gash in his leg.

Being removed by ambulance for treatment, the convoy was stopped by cannon fire that rendered the road impassable. Bullard and the other wounded members of the 170th spent the day and the night in the ambulance, immobile, until the road could be sufficiently repaired for them to proceed. On March 7, 1916, Bullard arrived at Bar-le-Duc. Hundreds of wounded were marshalled together and loaded on trains to Lyons, to the Hotel Dieu, a hospital. The trip took three days, as the train stopped occasionally to offload soldiers who had died, or to get local treatment for those who needed immediate care.

Bullard convalesced for three months. Doctors expected him to never walk again without assistance, assuming he would always limp even if he could walk. Bullard, of course, called their bet. Toward the end of his hospitalization it was announced that he would receive the prestigious *Croix de Guerre*, for his heroism in saving his buddies. Bullard wanted to walk and stand erect for the ceremony and redoubled his efforts to rehabilitate.

During his extended convalescence, Bullard met a Commandant Ferrolino, who, it turns out, was the head of the French Flying Service at Brun. When asked what Bullard wanted to do once he was healed, he told Ferrolino that he wanted to be a gunner for the Air Service. Commandant Ferrolino helped to make his application a reality and Bullard arrived at Caz-au-lac on October 6, 1916, for air gunnery training.

While there, Bullard ran into a former Foreign Legionnaire and fellow American, Edmond Genet. He knew Genet from his infantry days, and found out that Genet was training to be a pilot in the squadron known as the Lafayette Escadrille. As the United States had remained neutral in the conflict, any Americans fighting for the French were doing so in volunteer units. Early in the war the American aviator volunteers were formed into the American Flying Corps as a unit separate from the French flyers. As the war drew on, volunteers were integrated into French squadrons. Because of U.S. neutrality, the name was quickly changed to the Lafayette Escadrille. After training, that is where Bullard would wind up.

In between Bullard's acceptance into the Air Services and the beginning of his training, he dined with a couple of American expatriates in Paris. Telling them he intended to become a pilot, one of the men bet Bullard $2000.00, a tidy sum in 1916, he would never succeed. As this chapter obviously continues, Bullard won the bet.

Returning to aerial machine gunner training, Bullard made a formal request to his commander to be considered for pilot training. He learned to fire a machine gun from the back of a moving truck and from a moving motorboat, all to simulate what he might encounter in the rear seat of an airplane. He got to fire at real airplanes, too, but using a camera shaped like a machine gun. After a few weeks, his orders to report for pilot training came through.

Pilot training in those days was quite different than today. Whereas a budding military pilot learns to fly in ever more complex aircraft while a qualified instructor rides along, in 1916 it was hands on and solo. After basic ground instructions, a pilot was assigned to a Bleriot *"Peguin"*, French for penguin. The *Peguin* was a plane with the wings clipped so that it could not actually leave the ground.

Many early airplanes were equipped with something called a rotary engine. This type of engine arranges the cylinders around a central crankshaft, like more modern radial engines, which facilitates air cooling and concentrates the mass longitudinally. Unlike a radial engine, however, the propeller is attached to crankcase and cylinders while the crankshaft remains stationary. Essentially, the entire engine spins with the propeller. This creates an interesting and potentially dangerous situation.

The axle of a spinning gyroscope wants to remain stable and at a right angle to the rotation. When the axle is forced to change its orientation precession occurs. You can see the result of this if you spin a top. As the center of rotation moves a little, the top starts to wobble, moving at right angles to the direction of spin.

Now picture a heavy, rapidly spinning engine and propeller combination attached to the front of an airplane that uses a tail skid to move it around on the ground. As thrust gets the plane moving and speed increases the horizontal stabilizer lifts the tail off the ground. This causes a change in the orientation of the engine's axis. Depending on the direction of rotation, the plane will be under pressure to turn left or right. All pilots of propeller-driven, single engine airplanes learn to overcome this by steering in the opposite direction as required. That correction is required as the propeller is acting as a gyroscope. Now multiply that by the mass of the entire engine and you can see how difficult it might be to control.

Bullard's first experience with the *Peguin* required him to start the engine, give it gas, and, with the tail off the ground as if on a takeoff roll, taxi the plane in a straight line. Of course, as the plane began to pick up speed it began to swerve left. Bullard pressed on the rudder pedals to try to compensate, but having no real feel for the controls, the plane overcorrected to the right, and then back to the left more violently, and on, until he wound up going in circles. Embarrassed, he got some comfort in watching his fellow trainees go through the same thing. It is noted that one of his peers wound up ground looping his *Peguin* and had to be extracted from an upside down craft.

Like all trainee pilots that eventually got into the air, Bullard learned the intricacies of flying ever more powerful and capable airplanes. Bullard found that if he turned left the nose of the plane would try to pitch upward, and a right turn had the opposite effect. Good pilots in the Great War learned to use this bit of physics to their advantage when maneuvering in combat.

Bullard's final check flight required him to fly aerial maneuvers at two thousand feet, make two passes over the airfield, lower the nose for final approach, and cut his engine in order to glide to a landing at a pre-determined spot. He flew the plan well until it was time to land. Not being able to remember whether to lower the nose, then cut the power, or vice versa, Bullard circled the field several times. His decision became clear when the airplane ran out of fuel and he had to glide to what appears to have been a landing good enough to warrant his graduation. He was issued Pilot Certificate #6950 on May 5, 1917.

After a six-day leave during which Bullard picked up his $2000.00 winnings, Bullard went to advanced training. There, in a series of higher and higher performance machines, he learned aerial battle techniques and aerobatic maneuvers. He qualified to fly a two-engine Caudron bombing and observation plane along with a variety of single engine trainers and fighters.

Bullard encountered another roadblock to his ambitions. A certain Dr. Edmund Gros, an American, a commissioned major, had been instrumental in setting up the Lafayette Escadrille. Of the 22 pilots that graduated with Bullard from advanced training, he was left waiting while all of the others were assigned to combat duty. While the French were well known for treating everyone equally, without regard to skin color, Gros was an American. From engaging in petty activities like withholding Bullard's paycheck until after the banks closed so he couldn't cash it for the weekend, to doing everything he could to keep Bullard from getting assigned to combat duty, Dr. Gros kept Bullard on hold for nearly three months.

Bullard complained to his commander, but was told he could do nothing about it. Apparently, someone intervened, though (it doesn't seem to be recorded as to whom) and Bullard got orders to report. Gros ensured that the Lafayette Escadrille stayed white, though, and Bullard was assigned to Escadrille Spa-93, a French unit.

The airplane he was assigned was a SPAD-VII. Built by *Société Pour L'Aviation et ses Dérivés*, it had a cowl-mounted machine gun was synchronized to fire through the propeller arc, so the pilot aimed the entire plane when attacking a target. Its V-8 Hispano-Suiza engine made 150 horsepower. With a top speed of 125 miles per hour it was much faster than any of the planes in which Bullard had learned to fly.

As was the technology of the time, the plane was made of wood and covered in fabric. The fabric was coated with a type of paint called dope, which shrunk and tightened the fabric and made it rigid, and water- and fuel proof. The front portion of the plain was clad in sheet metal surrounding the engine. The use of a V-8 engine reduced the airplane's tendency to yaw wildly when direction changed, as was the case with the rotary engine planes in which Bullard trained.

After receiving his assignment, Bullard got to spend another few days in Paris. Soldiers destined for the front were routinely feted by locals, so he had a great time while everyone else picked up the tab. While in Paris he met a mademoiselle who had an unusual pet, a rhesus monkey. When

Bullard reported to advanced training, the monkey, whom he named "Jimmy", went with him.

He spent his first couple of weeks at Spa-93 with his assigned mechanics getting to know the airplane, his crew, and practicing flying maneuvers. The SPAD was not as maneuverable as some contemporary airplanes, but it was fast and streamlined. It was capable of reaching nearly 250 miles per hour in a dive. As the war drew on, specific tactics were developed to take advantage of the airplane's high-speed capabilities.

Bullard's first combat flight came in September, 1917. Along with Jimmy the monkey, he was a part of a formation of 14 SPAD VII and Nieuport fighter planes flying from an airstrip near Verdun. At 6,000 feet, the planes formed into a "V" formation, with the lead taken by a Captain Pisard. Two groups of six planes formed the "wings" of the "V", with a single plane in trail.

The flight took them to the edge of the battle line, with all eyes on the lookout for enemy aircraft. About a half hour in, Pisard signaled a turn that would take them across no-man's land and into German-held territory.

Bullard with Jimmy the Monkey

In the distance they could see German observation balloons and airplanes. Occasionally a puff of gray smoke would indicate ground fire from anti-aircraft guns. Below, Bullard could see the trenches that he had so recently escaped as a wounded infantryman. He would have had very little time to contemplate his past, though, as he needed to keep his eyes off the ground, and out of the cockpit, looking for enemy aircraft.

Captain Pisard suddenly signaled the formation to battle maneuvers by banking hard to one side. All of the planes broke off and started to hunt for the incoming enemy, going off in every direction in order to keep opposing pilots from being able to target them.

Bullard's heart must have been racing. This was his first taste of aerial combat. But where was the enemy? Still searching, Bullard saw Pisard fly past him and signal the squadron to join back up. There was no attack, just an initiation rite that all of the new pilots got put through. Back on the ground, all was explained, and Bullard was congratulated for his surviving the hazing.

He had no time to revel in his success, though, as the squadron was flying two sorties per day, leaving him just enough time for some quick rest, and back to cockpit.

While Bullard didn't record how many days had elapsed, it wasn't long before he tasted real air combat. Bullard's squadron was ordered into the air and toward the front at Verdun. Fourteen aviators and one simian copilot, Jimmy. As before, the planes formed a "V" at 6,000 feet and, as they crossed the lines they spotted four large German bombers and a 16-plane escort of Fokker Dr.1 triplanes. Commander Victor Ménard, leading the formation, signaled the attack. The flight broke into two 7-plane groups as the German fighters dove at them, machine guns blazing.

Imagine Bullard, working his control stick and rudder pedals doing everything he could to avoid becoming a target. The rat-a-tat of machine gun fire, aircraft turning, rolling and looping all around, the smell and feel of hot castor oil blowing back from the engine all created an almost overwhelming palette of sensations.

Bullard records seeing one of the bombers trailing smoke, and two of the Fokkers damaged and headed toward crashes. He got behind a Fokker and managed to squeeze off some rounds from his machine gun, but didn't know whether any rounds hit. Then he was the prey, and as bullets whizzed past above his cockpit he put his SPAD into a spiraling dive. When he recovered he had a Fokker ahead and above him, took aim, and fired. The Fokker jerked and spiraled out of range but Bullard didn't know whether his fire had hit home.

Bullard watched as a German bomber, trailing smoke, began to turn for the safety of the German lines. A German fighter flew in front of him, blocking his view, and after it flew by he saw the bomber erupt into flames and break up.

Another Fokker flew into his range and he ripped off a few more rounds almost instinctively. He saw the other three bombers spiraling toward the ground, two of them trailing flame and smoke.

The remaining German fighters broke off and returned to the east, to safety. The whole episode lasted barely two minutes. Bullard, with time to reflect, discovered he was gripping the control stick much tighter than usual. On the flight home he forced himself to relax and consider what he just experienced.

Back at the landing field and tied down, the pilots gathered for a post-combat debriefing. The squadron lost two pilots, which Bullard failed to notice until the commandant made the announcement. And, then, his mechanics let him know that he had fired 78 rounds, and his plane came home with seven bullet holes in the tail section. Close!

The flight schedule on the bulletin board had him back in the air between 7 and 9 the next morning, and 1 and 3 in the afternoon. This schedule of two 2-hour flights continued, day in and day out, unless weather grounded the planes.

On September 13, 1917, Bullard was transferred from Spa-93 to Spa-85. It had air jurisdiction for the section around Vadalaincourt and Bar-le-Duc. One day while patrolling this sector Bullard and his squadron encountered a flight of aggressive Fokker Dr.1 triplanes who headed straight for them with the intent to engage. His squadron leader signaled combat maneuvers, and the SPADs and Nieuports scattered, rolled and spun to try to gain position on the Fokkers.

Bullard was closing head-on with one of the Germans. Seeing the flash of machinegun fire he stepped on his right rudder pedal and started to spiral downward, out of range, and out of the German's sights. When he recovered and pulled up he found another Fokker in his sights. He fired some short bursts as the German pilot tried to shake him. Bullard had him, punching a line of holes in the triplane's wings and fuselage. Fabric tore loose from the German airplane, as its engine started to cough and belch smoke.

The German turned toward enemy territory with Bullard in pursuit, until Bullard saw the trails of machine gun tracer bullets coming from the ground. In pursuing the Fokker, he had flown near the ground, making him a target for German gunners in the trenches. Bullard saw holes appearing in the fabric of the plane and heard the metallic ping of bullets hitting vital parts. His controls became mushy. He turned for friendly lines and lost sight of the wounded triplane, never learning whether he had scored a kill.

Nursing his plane back into French territory his engine started to spew smoke and castor oil, signaling it didn't have much more to give. One final "thunk" and the engine died entirely. Bullard put the plane on the ground in the no-man's land between the opposing forces. All the while, German infantrymen and machine gunners kept firing at him. Even though the landing was on muddy, uneven ground, Bullard managed to "keep the shiny side up", even if the shiny side was covered in torn cloth and castor oil from the motor.

Bullard jumped from the cockpit, taking Jimmy, and took refuge on the side of the plane away from the German gunfire. For hours, Bullard and Jimmy hunkered down on the cold, wet ground contemplating how to get back to French lines while bullets continued to pierce his SPAD.

When dusk fell, the constant gunfire stopped, and Bullard heard voices coming out of the forest toward him. From full alert, he went to a feeling of relief when the voices were heard to be speaking French. Soldiers, horses, and squadron mechanics emerged from the trees and were pleased to find the pilot and his passenger, still alive and well. They dragged the wounded plane to safety and then removed the wings. The plane and the wings were loaded onto a cart and carried back to the airfield. They counted 96 holes in the airplane, but, fortunately, none in Bullard.

Bullard had encountered the pilots of the German *Jasta* 4, 6, 10 and 11 of the *Jagdgeschwade Eine* (JG-1). This unit was better known to many as "The Flying Circus", and was commanded by Manfred von Richthofen, *der Rote Baron*, the infamous Red Baron.

September turned into October, and, weather permitting, Bullard and his fellow pilots flew two sorties a day. On a particularly cold, cloudy and nasty morning, Bullard awoke, looked outside, and went back to sleep. No flying in this weather.

He was awakened by the duty sergeant later in the morning and told to get ready to fly at 11 AM. Spots of blue sky were appearing amongst the clouds and the weather, while cold and windy, was improving.

Bullard put on his flight suit and all of the cold-weather gear he could muster. Jimmy had been very quiet that morning and appeared to be ailing. Bullard let him stay behind as he mounted his SPAD, taxied out, took off and climbed to 12,000 feet with his 16-ship squadron.

Dodging clouds, Bullard emerged from behind one to find he had lost sight of the rest of the flight. He got a clear look at the ground below and found he had crossed the Verdun battlefield and into German territory. With no other aircraft nearby he could hear only the sound of his own engine and the wind over the wings and through the wires holding them together. He scanned the sky looking for his wingmen when he spotted a "V" formation well ahead and about 3,000 feet below his altitude. His first thought, according to his memoirs, was that he had found his missing comrades. It occurred to him they were going the wrong direction, though.

German planes! Seven Pfalz biplanes were getting closer, but did not seem to be taking any actions that would indicate they had spotted Bullard. Bulllard flew into the nearest cloud cover, freezing cold and wet, to avoid detection. When he emerged he found that the Pfalz scout planes had passed by and below him. Bullard saw a chance for a victory and spun his plane around and into a dive toward the German formation.

Bullard took aim on the trailing plane in the formation, cocked his Vickers machine gun, and let lose several rounds. Apparently startled by the sound of gunfire and the tracer bullets flying past him, the German pilot turned his head to see Bullard's SPAD closing fast. The German pulled back on his stick and put his plane into a loop, intending to let Bullard's speed carry him past and to come out on Bullard's tail.

Bullard executed a hard right bank and dove for the cover of a nearby cloud. When the German recovered from his loop, expecting to see the SPAD ahead, it was nowhere to be found. When Bullard emerged into clear air, the Pfalz was above him and crossing from left to right. Bullard recalls he could see the Black cross on the fuselage, as he raised the nose, added power, and took aim. Bullets marched along the side of the Pfalz to the cockpit. The pilot jerked suddenly and the plane began a spiral descent toward the ground.

Before the other Pfalz pilots could react, Bullard flew back into a cloud, changed direction, and headed for home. While his first kill in September could not be independently confirmed, there was no such issue with this one. The plane went down in French territory.

While Bullard flew more missions in the autumn of 1917, American racism effectively ended his flying career soon after his first confirmed victory. In April, 1917, the United States had declared war on Germany and entered the conflict. The first American troops under its flag arrived in September. The Americans set about developing their own flying corps, in many cases using pilots from the Lafayette Flying Corps.

Bullard applied for a transfer to the U.S. Army Air Corps, passed a required physical in spite of obstacles thrown in front of him, and awaited orders to be transferred. That transfer never came. Apparently the same Dr. Gros who tried to hinder his career before his acceptance by the French ensured that Bullard would not fly under American colors.

Not long after his rejection by the U.S. Army, Bullard got orders via the French flight surgeon evacuating him from combat based upon the injury to his leg suffered when he was in infantryman. As a good soldier, Bullard was forced to accept, ending his time as a pilot.

Bullard went on to an eclectic life in Paris. Over the years between the wars, he owned and ran a successful bistro, and, later, an athletic club and boxing gym. For a time he used his fluency in German to spy on German agents who were customers at his restaurant, working with the French Resistance. He married, and had two daughters.

He returned to the United States in July, 1940, as the Germans took over France and made his continued existence there a sketchy proposition. In America, he got quickly reacquainted with racism, but carried on. All of this is worth reading another time, as this essay seeks to cover his life as "The World's First Black Fighter Pilot", the phrase he kept on his *carte de visite* until he died in 1961.

Eugene Bullard and Dave Garroway on The Today Show

On September 14, 1994 Eugene Jacques Bullard received a posthumous promotion to Second Lieutenant in the United States Air Force. This was the promotion that was refused in 1917 that resulted in his never flying as an American aviator.

CRAIG S. MARCKWARDT

CHAPTER 4 - FROM BESSIE TO WILLA

Unknown to most of us, women of color have been part of the aviation scene since the days following the end of hostilities in Europe in 1918. The first woman of color to hold a pilot's license of any kind was African-American and Native American by heritage. In her shadow, others would overcome incredible barriers to continue her legacy.

At one end of this continuum is Bessie Coleman. She received her international pilot's license in France in 1921. She also personifies the singular focus and dedication that seems to overtake the people who defy the established norms and prejudices and, ultimately, reach their dreams.

In 1937, Willa Brown became the first African-American woman to earn a U.S. issued pilot's license. Like Bessie Coleman, she overcame tremendous obstacles to find her way into the sky. Janet Harmon Bragg received the first U.S. commercial pilot certificate issued to a Black woman in 1943 in Chicago, but only after being turned down by an examiner in Alabama.

Between these pioneers, many other women of color had roles in the advancement of aviation in the Black community. We need to start at the beginning, though.

Bessie Coleman

Elizabeth "Bessie" Coleman was born in 1892 or 1893 (depending on the source), the tenth child of sharecroppers in rural Atlanta, Texas. When she was two years old, her parents moved the family to Waxahachie, Texas where they and her older brothers, worked in the cotton fields. Though her parents were illiterate, young Bessie, aged six, apparently showed an aptitude for reading and math, and enrolled in the one school in town available for African-American children. In spite of annual interruptions in schooling during the cotton harvest, she completed all of the eight grades taught at the school. Her performance as a student was such that she applied to, and was accepted by a Baptist Missionary Church School on scholarship, allowing her to complete high school.

In 1901, Coleman's father left the family and moved to Indian Territory (now a part of Oklahoma) for better financial opportunities. When she turned eighteen, Bessie left Texas and enrolled in the Oklahoma Colored Agricultural and Normal University in Langston City, a little northeast of Oklahoma City. After a year, however, her money ran out and she returned to Waxahachie.

In 1916 Coleman went to Chicago, Illinois, moving in with one of her brothers. This got her away from the agrarian, oppressive post-reconstruction conditions of the South and into the urban, although still racially segregated, African-American community in Chicago. She took a job as a manicurist in a shop that catered to white men, some of whom were pilots who returned from the war in Europe with stories about flying and airplanes. It was there that Coleman decided she wanted to fly, and even took a second job to raise money faster so she could take lessons.

She made friends in Chicago, most notably an attorney named Robert Abbott. In 1905, Abbott founded the *Chicago Defender*, a newspaper for the Black community. Beginning as a hand printed paper produced in the boarding house where Abbott lived, it grew to become arguably the most important, and certainly, the most widely circulated African-American newspaper in the country, topping 125,000 readers by the time Coleman moved to Chicago, and over 200,000 by the early 1920's. *The Defender*, distributed in large part by Black railroad porters on trains bound across the United States, was credited with much of the "Great Migration" that saw African-Americans from the South, streaming to Chicago for greater financial opportunity and less social discrimination.

As an adherent to the Baha'I Faith, Abbott stressed his beliefs that racial prejudice had no place in America, or in the world, generally. His newspaper stressed this tenet, and worked to improve the social and economic status of Black people across the country.

Of course, at this time, no flight school in Chicago, or in the U.S. for that matter, would accept a female student, much less a woman of color. It was Abbott who encouraged, and sponsored, Coleman's eventual move to France. As pioneering pilot Eugene Bullard discovered a decade earlier, France did not discriminate on the basis of color, and had become, arguably, the epicenter of aircraft development and the promotion of aviation.

Not only did she raise the money to travel to France, but she learned to speak the language. After learning from the famous pilots and aircraft designers, the Caudron brothers, Coleman received her *Fédération Aéronautique Internationale* (FAI) flying license on June 15, 1921. She spent time in Europe honing her flying skills and learning to parachute. While in the Netherlands, She had occasion to meet Anthony Fokker, arguably one of the best and most prolific airplane designers and manufacturers. She even received additional flight training from the Fokker Company's chief pilot.

This was in the heyday, the so called "Golden Age of Aviation", the period after the Great War that saw the rise of barnstorming and records for higher, faster, and farther being set by pilots worldwide. Coleman realized that, with commercial aviation still on the horizon, the way to make a living flying and to fulfill her promise to herself "to amount to something", her path would be exhibition flying. In 1922, Coleman returned to the U.S., settling first in New York. Described as intelligent, beautiful, and well-spoken, she took up public speaking in schools, churches and theaters advocating for Black interest in the booming field of aviation. The press adored her and covered her activities. It has been said that she padded her accomplishments a bit, but she became known in the African-American community as "Queen Bess".

In 1923 she had saved enough to buy her first plane. With having established her credentials as a pilot her ultimate goal was to open a flight school for African-Americans. Things began shakily as when, departing New York for the West Coast to participate in an air show, she crashed her plane and damaged it sufficiently to be rendered no longer flyable. She spent three months in hospital, returning to Chicago to recover and regroup.

It took her a year and a half, but she found herself flying barnstorming shows in Texas. Between her flying and personal appearances, she earned enough for a new plane, a Curtis JN-4 "Jenny". The Jenny was the American-built biplane that, since its introduction in 1915, had become the primary trainer for nearly all American, and numerous British, pilots throughout the First World War and after. With the end of hostilities, surplus JN-4's were plentiful, relatively reliable, affordable, and were used by barnstormers and airmail fliers extensively.

By 1925, Coleman had found steady work as an exhibition pilot and parachutist, as well as a celebrity speaker. She wrote to a sister that she was finally going to earn enough money to make her flying school a reality. By then, she was being called "Brave Bessie" in the press.

At the end of April, 1926, Coleman's fellow pilot and mechanic, William D. Wells, after a show in Orlando, Florida left to fly the "Jenney" to Jacksonville to do an exhibition to support the Jacksonville Negro Welfare League, while Coleman travelled by rail. Ominously, Wells had to make three unintentional stops to repair the airplane in order to get to the event, scheduled for May 1.

On April 30, the pair flew over the site to survey a location for her to perform a parachute jump. In the cockpit while Wells piloted, Coleman was not belted into her seat so she could see easily over the sides. According to witnesses, at about 1000 feet above ground, the plane suddenly nosedived and rolled over, throwing Coleman out. The plane then crashed, and both Coleman and Wells died at the scene. The cause is thought to be a wrench that was left out of place and jammed the controls.

"Brave Bessie" had three funerals, one each in Jacksonville, Orlando and Chicago. It is reported that ten thousand mourners attended in Chicago. Outside the Black community it took years for her story to spread, but spread it has. What was perhaps the first flight academy run by, and for African-Americans, opened in Los Angeles, bore her name, and was dedicated to her memory.

The group called the Bessie Coleman Aero Clubs was established in 1929 and actively recruited students both male and female. Its history is covered in a subsequent chapter. The group's first woman pilot trainee recruited was Florence Reeves. We know little about her except that Clubs' founder William Powell described her as "...a very adept student, progressing most amazingly in her ground work, especially navigation, and doing fine in her flying, too." However, she left the group in a snit over rumors that another budding female aviator would be joining to take her place. While the rumors were unfounded, she pulled out of an event involving Oscar de Priest, at the time the only African-American member of Congress, at the last moment and she dropped off the radar entirely as far as can be determined. Marie Dickerson was an actress, singer, and dancer who had moved to Los Angeles hoping to find a Hollywood career. She was, according to the *Los Angeles Times*, a frequent headliner at Frank Sebastian's Cotton Club in Culver City, California, and a frequent visitor to Mines Field and the Bessie Coleman Aero Clubs. When Florence Reeves decided to sabotage the christening of the "Oscar de Priest" airplane for the group, she jumped in and, dressed in flying togs and accompanied by actress Mable Norman, escorted the Congressman and his retinue, while a member of the club's executive board, Susie Hancock broke the champagne bottle on the propeller spinner and made the name official.

Ms. Dickerson began her aviator studies then, and became a skilled navigator and an accomplished pilot. William Powell (founder of the Bessie Coleman Aero Clubs) describes her first flight as a navigator, from Lincoln Avenue Airfield in Los Angeles to San Diego in the Aero Clubs' American Eagle biplane. The route required her to plot two legs, first to Oceanside, California, and then to San Diego, using the airplane's compass and drift indicator, a watch and maps indicating magnetic variation. Taking what she had learned in ground school in classes at the club, she plotted a path that took the flyers directly to the waypoint and on to the destination with, essentially, no error. The flight out was in clear air, so her calculations could easily be checked by observation. On the return flight, however, before reaching Los Angeles a thick layer of low clouds set in, totally obscuring the ground. Given where they needed to go, an error in plotting could have but the aviators out over the Pacific Ocean, or into mountains. In either case, the result could have been disastrous. As it happened, she nailed the course, though they could not locate the airfield through the fog. When a clear patch opened up, the pilot, Herman Banning found a newly planted, flat orange grove and set the airplane down safely. The total damage was to two small trees, costing the Bessie Coleman Aero Clubs $25 to assuage the farmer. Without Ms. Dickerson's skills the result could have been much worse.

Marie Dickerson, interviewed near the end of her 84 year life, is quoted as saying, "The old planes were made out of wood and nylon – I don't even think it was nylon. And we just took chances flying around."

She was featured, along with six male counterparts in what may be the largest gathering of people of color to witness an airshow in history in December, 1931. While Marie Dickerson Coker lived until 1990, it appears that her flying career ended with that of Powell's "Five Blackbirds" (there were actually seven pilots that day), a victim of the Great Depression of the 1930's.

Janet Bragg was born Jane Nettie Harmon in Griffin, Georgia in 1907. (She became "Janet" when she decided to combine her two aunt's namesakes, Jane and Nettie, to make it easier in school to write on the chalkboard.) Like Bessie Coleman, she had both African-American and Native American ancestry. She attended an Episcopal high school and then Spellman College in Atlanta, Georgia, a school founded in 1924 as an all-female, Black Baptist institution.

Janet Harmon Bragg

After graduating with her nursing credential in 1929 she moved to Chicago, Illinois, and went to work for the Wilson Hospital. Married, and then divorced a couple of years later, she held increasingly more demanding and prestigious nursing and administrative positions while continuing her education. Eventually, she went to work for physicians in private practice while attending Loyola University. She would wind up owning and running nursing homes and facilities in her later life.

Unlike many of the people in this book who seemed to feel the calling of aviation early in their lives, usually because of some sort of encounter as children with airplanes, Harmon's path to flight began well into her career as a nurse. She recounts in her autobiography of seeing a billboard in Chicago that depicted a momma bird nudging a baby bird out of nest, with the caption, "Birds learn to fly. Why can't you?" Struck with inspiration she began looking into where someone of color could, in fact, learn to fly. She made some inquiries, including to the *Chicago Defender*, the newspaper that had been so pivotal in Bessie Coleman's learning to fly.

In 1928, Harmon, then Janet Waterford, enrolled at the Curtiss-Wright School of Aeronautics in Chicago. The school would ultimately become The Aeronautical University, an all-Black school run by Curtiss-Wright graduates John C. Robinson and Cornelius Coffey. The Aeronautical University only offered courses in aircraft maintenance and the ground school requirements for a pilot's license.

Robinson, along with Harmon, would later become the driving force behind the acceptance of Black aviators into the Civilian Pilot Training Program. The CPTP was organized as war was approaching in order to ensure a supply of combat pilots should the United States become involved. Initially, with CPTP accepting only white applicants, the pair lobbied important people in local, state and the federal government, resulting in a CPTP at Chicago's Harlem Airport, and later, the one that was formed at Robinson's alma mater, the Tuskegee Institute in the late 1930's. Robinson has been called "The Father of The Tuskegee Airmen"

.

Cornelius Coffey opened the first non-university affiliated aviation school for pilots of color, and was, subsequently, married to Willa Brown. More on these pioneers follow in a later chapter.

Sandwiching in aviation coursework between her nursing activities, Harmon spent each Tuesday and Thursday evening studying everything from aeronautics to meteorology to aircraft maintenance to civil aviation laws and regulations. The first woman to enroll, among a couple of dozen students, Harmon had to learn what tool was used for what job, and, as the school didn't have enough tools to go around, she bought herself a set of basic items and green tool box. She said she had the tool box, and, at least, a few of the tools from those days, for the rest of her life.

The Aeronautical University did not have any airplanes. Having completed all of the ground school work, Harmon was ready to take actual flying lessons. Robinson and Coffey had an airplane that was kept at field in Melrose Park. A white pilot and instructor at the field, one "Dynamite" Anderson, charged her $15 per hour for instruction in his Travel Air.

The class of student pilots at Aeronautical University decided to form a group, becoming the Challenger Air Pilots' Association to further their chances of success. Most airfields limited access to Black pilots, so they decided to buy land and build their own. A suitable amount of acreage was secured in the all-Black community of Robbins. The group, often with assistance of local residents who were excited about the prospect of their own airport, cleared the land, laid down a runway surfaced with railroad coal cinders, and built a hangar.

Still needing an airplane, Harmon bought a red, open cockpit, three place International for $500. The plane had basic instrumentation; a tachometer, an altimeter, and a compass, and dual controls so it could be used for training. Coffey and Robinson picked up the plane from the seller and delivered it to the airport just in time for winter to set in. The plane stayed in the hangar, being started and maintained by Coffey, until things thawed in the spring of 1933.

At that point, Harmon began learning to fly in earnest. After ten hours of instruction from Coffey, she flew solo. So did the remaining ten other students and members of the Challenger Air Pilots' Association. She continued flying as often as she could, as it was her airplane, and amassed thirty-five solo hours, including the required three hour cross country. Using road maps and railroad routes which were much more comprehensive than the fairly rudimentary aerial charts then available she flew from Robbins to Joliet, then onto South Chicago before returning to Robbins.

Ready to test, Robinson accompanied Harmon to Pal-Waukee Airport north of Chicago, where she presented herself to a white federal flight examiner. "It doesn't matter what color you are. Just that you know what you are doing", he told her. And she did, and passed with no problem, becoming a licensed pilot.

The airport in Robbins was small, with a single runway angled northwest to southeast, favoring the prevailing winds. Departure to the southeast took pilots low over the adjacent white neighborhood in Midlothian, which was a source of irritation to the homeowners. The issue resolved itself when during the winter the hangar collapsed under heavy snow. The club negotiated space at the Harlem Field, which had better facilities, and that became their base of operations throughout the period up to and through World War II.

Harmon next bought a three place, yellow Piper Cub Cruiser monoplane with an enclosed cabin. She, accompanied by a male Challenger pilot/mechanic and his wife, flew home to Atlanta to attend the Graduate Nurses Association conference. Equipped with a radio, an oddity at the time, she recalled contacting Chandler Field in Atlanta for landing procedures. The airport operator who spoke to her on the radio was curious to see a woman pilot, but was "speechless" when he saw that she was Black.

By this time, the *Guardian* had dubbed her "The Flying Nurse". She was becoming well known, although her mother, who now lived with her in Chicago, new nothing of her aviation activities until a friend told her about them. This led to Harmon taking her mother to Harlem Field, now the home of the Challenger Air Pilots' Association. She asked her mother if she was willing to fly, after letting her sit in the parked airplane, and then taxiing out to the runway. She recounted her mother saying, "If anything happened to you, I'd die anyway". So, with that, Harmon took her flying, and, apparently, her mother enjoyed it very much.

As war in Europe threatened to engulf the world, the federal government relented and allowed a Civilian Pilot Training Program school in Chicago run by Challenger pilots. John Robinson had, for years, tried to convince the administration of his alma mater, The Tuskegee Institute, to develop a training program for aviators of color, but to no avail. With war looming, however, a second CPTP was established there. C. Alfred "Chief" Anderson was the head instructor, going on to take a significant role in the establishment and training of the "Tuskegee Airmen".

In Chicago, Harmon and Charles Johnson established another flight school to meet the needs of aspiring pilots not eligible for Coffey's CPTP, usually because of age. Their school had both white and Black students, including three white women. One of these brought in a letter and application for an organization called the Woman's Airforce Service Pilots, or WASPs. With men off flying combat missions the WASP was formed to take on non-combat roles, including delivering and ferrying aircraft around the country, and even to Europe.

Harmon filled out an application, and she and her white female students all received telegrams from one Ethel Sheehy asking that they come to the Palmer House in Chicago for interviews. Prophetically, the Black doorman directed her to the servant elevator at the back of the building, and Harmon had to explain to the doorman that she was a pilot and there at the invitation of Mrs. Sheehy.

Arriving at the suite of rooms being used for the applicant interviews, Harmon was the last to interview. Sheehy asked if Harmon was a pilot and then told her that she, "had never interviewed a colored girl before." Sheehy told her that the WASP training was to be conducted in Sweetwater, Texas, apparently hoping the idea of going south would not appeal to Harmon. Finally, Sheehy said she would need to refer Harmon's application to Jacqueline Cochran, the commander of the WASPs, "at headquarters".

Not surprisingly, her three students were all accepted into the organization, but Cochran's telegram to Harmon said that, "whatever Mrs. Sheehy told you still stands."

Soon after, the *Chicago Tribune* ran an article stating that the military was looking for 6,000 nurses. Her application was met with, "the quota for colored nurses is filled."

In February, 1943, anxious to improve her flying skills, and with the CPTP footing most of the bill, Harmon took a leave of absence from her job at a funeral insurance firm, and flew a borrowed red Piper Cub Cruiser from Chicago to Tuskegee. With her was flight instructor Walter Robinson and a student pilot, Manuella Jackson.

Their first scheduled fuel stop was to be in Huntsville, Alabama, but strong headwinds forced them to land in a field near the town of Boaz, Alabama, out of fuel. Attracting some attention with the landing, Harmon asked if anyone could direct them to a gas station. During that period of time, gas was rationed because of the war, and purchasing it required the use of ration coupons. The trio had several, as the club had pooled resources to ensure the success of the flight and the mission.

A young white man with a pickup truck and a five gallon gas can, offered to drive them into town. They got their high octane auto fuel and got back to the plane. With only a half hour until sunset, Harmon asked if anyone in the crowd that had gathered could direct them to a Black family where they might be able to spend the night. The fellow who answered told her, "Naw, we are pretty tough on n*****s around here."

Harmon managed to keep Robinson from becoming upset and combative and they decided that departing was the best way to avoid a confrontation or a lynching. They added the gas to the plane, and took off for Huntsville only another few minutes away.

They found an old landing strip used by the Army Air Corps for refueling, and set the plane down. The white gentleman who provided the fuel also gave them the name of James Smith, a recently widowed Black man with a large house and just himself to occupy it. He apparently not only welcomed the company, but made sure that the flyers were well fed. In her autobiography Harmon describes a real Southern meal, including liver and onions, rice and cabbage, and homemade bread. When morning came they awoke to ham and scrambled eggs, hot biscuits and honey, and coffee and milk.

Mr. Smith refused their offer of payment, but they left something behind for him when they set off to get back to the airplane. Fueled up, with ideal flying weather, the happy travelers resumed their flight to Tuskegee.

The CPTP was located at Kennedy Airport. The airfield at the Tuskegee Institute, and nearby Moton Field, were both being used exclusively by the military training the pilots who would soon see action in Europe. It apparently took some searching to locate Kennedy, but when they landed they were greeted by none other than C. Alfred "Chief" Anderson, the head instructor for the Tuskegee Airmen.

For several weeks, Harmon flew with many of the same instructors that trained the fighter pilots at Moton and Tuskegee. Daily flights perfected maneuvers such as chandelles, spins and lazy eights, each session was carefully debriefed on the ground.

When "Chief" felt she was ready, he sent her to Birmingham Alabama to take her written test for her commercial pilot's certificate. She had already passed it once in Chicago, but too much time had passed to have it apply to her final certification. Once again, being in the South reared its ugly head, as she had to take a bus to the state capital. In Alabama that meant that the only seat available to her as a Black woman was in the back row. Unfair as she saw that, there was reason to go along and just get the trip over with.

The federal flight examiner, T. K. Hudson, administered the written test and determined that she had passed. She returned to Tuskegee that evening to await her practical test, flying the airplane. Her flight instructor George Allen spent the time before the check ride to put her through every maneuver and situation that he thought she would be required to perform properly during her flight.

After a rainy day, when the weather was beautifully clear and calm, Hudson arrived by car and unloaded his parachute and proceeded with the exam. By law, parachutes were required for both the examiner and the pilot for this type of flight. Once in the air the flight went just as Allen had said it would, beginning with a power off, forced landing drill, and one maneuver after another. After each, Hudson gave her a "thumbs up", and Harmon felt her confidence rise. The flight ended with a perfect, three-point landing.

George Allen asked Hudson, "How did she do?" From her autobiography:

> *"With a long southern drawl I'll never forget, he answered, 'George, she gave me a good flight. I would put her up against any of your flight instructors. But I've never given a colored girl a commercial license, and I don't intend to start now.' He threw his parachute in his car and drove off."*

After spending some more time at Tuskegee, it was time return to Chicago and her job. On the way she set down in her hometown of Griffin, Georgia, where her niece was an executive director for the Girl Scouts, Black Division. After getting time with her friends and family she organized an air show with the proceeds going to the Girl Scouts there.

Back in Chicago, she made arrangements for another attempt at the flight test. This time, the examiner was a Texan named Ritter, and when she told him about the situation in Alabama, Ritter's drawl had her believing that she may be experiencing déjà vu. He said to her, "We shall see", and proceeded with the check ride. It involved all of the maneuvers and simulated emergencies that she had already handled in Alabama, and Harmon said she was just ready to get it over with and be turned down again.

This time, however, Mr. Ritter shook her hand, congratulated her, and told her to pick up her commercial license at Municipal Airport.

Janet Harmon went on to parlay her experience and grit into a life that included ownership of two nursing homes in Chicago and extensive travel as a nursing professional in Africa. She worked in Ethiopia for the Emperor Haile Selassie, and hosted Black exchange students in Chicago.

At one point she was featured in *Life Magazine*. She married again, and lived until 1993.

In 1932 Willa Brown, a high school teacher in Gary, Indiana, took a job as a social worker in Chicago. Feeling that economic opportunities for African-Americans in the 1930's were lacking, and having an activist streak, Brown studied for, and received a Master of Business Administration degree from Northwestern. About that time, she developed an interest in aviation and involved herself by taking instruction from John Robinson and Cornelius Coffey, just as had Janet Harmon.

Born in Glascow, Kentucky in 1906, Brown worked her way through the Indiana State Teachers College as a maid and by student teaching. She received her bachelor's degree in education in 1931. Unlike Janet Harmon Bragg, Brown did not leave an autobiography, but her accomplishments have been recorded in a plethora of articles and remembrances.

Attending the Curtiss Wright Aeronautical University, she began her journey to flight by earning a Master Mechanic Certificate in 1935. All the while, she was taking flying lessons from Robinson and Coffey. She was not the first American woman to earn her U.S. pilot's license, as several women, including Ann Morrow Lindbergh, the wife of the man who was the first to fly non-stop and solo across the Atlantic Ocean, had been certified. She passed her flight tests in 1937 and received the first U.S. Department of Commerce pilot certificate issued to a woman of color. Her Black predecessors who held licenses, such as Bessie Coleman, had received theirs in France.

Willa Brown Coffey

She was a tireless promoter of African-American involvement in aviation in the same spirit as William Powell. To promote an air show in 1936, she decided that she would go to the press instead of waiting for the press to come to her. Women rarely wore slacks in those days, but as an "aviatrix", in the same way that the "Five Blackbirds" woman aviators dressed, she appeared in the offices of Robert Abbott's *Chicago Defender* newspaper wearing a leather flight jacket, riding jodhpurs, and boots. Described by her contemporaries as "tall and beautiful", she managed to bring the newsroom to a stop and got her message across.

She got the attention of a reporter named Enoch P. Waters, who covered the air show. Waters went on to become the managing editor of the *Defender* in later years, and had a great impact on the African-American presence in aviation. The Curtis-Wright school had been purchased and rebranded as the Coffey School of Aeronautics by the time that Brown got her flying license. Enoch Waters involved himself in the quest for the advancement of Blacks in aviation, writing articles encouraging potential aviators to leave the Jim Crow south and come north to Chicago to learn to fly. He, along with Coffey, Brown, and a number of others incorporated themselves into a group called the

National Airmen Association of America (NAAA). Their charter adhered to the goal of promoting Black airmanship and involvement.

In 1938, Brown and Coffey participated in an airshow at Harlem Airport, Chicago that drew some 30,000 people. This success, along with that of his flying school resulted in the Coffey School being awarded the first Civilian Pilot Training Program charter for pilots of color.

In 1939, Brown married Cornelius Coffey.

Between then, and 1940, Brown, already a board member and shareholder in the NAAA, also became involved in the Challenger Air Pilots' Association, the group that had built its own airport in Robbins, Illinois when no other airport would accept Black flyers. Members included Janet Harmon and John Robinson, along with Coffey and Brown. She became involved with the Chicago Girls' Flying Club, an organization seeking to gain acceptance for women aviators as a resource in times of strife and war, a very real prospect in the 1930's.

Brown became an instructor at Coffey's CPTP at Harlem Airport and taught at Wendell Phillips High School, both U.S. Civil Aviation Administration programs. Having attained both a commercial pilot certificate and her master mechanic license she was able to give instruction to literally hundreds of men and women, including many who would become members of the Army Air Forces training program at Tuskegee, and who would go on to fly and fight with distinction in Europe in World War II.

In 1941, the mayor of New York, Fiorello LaGuardia was the Director of the Office of Civilian Defense. Seeing the potential for the role of private pilots in times of domestic emergency, he signed into existence the Civil Air Patrol. Brown applied to join and in 1941 was commissioned as a second lieutenant, the first Black officer in the CAP. With her connection to the CPTP, she was named the federal coordinator of the CAP wing in Chicago. She was also named Coordinator of War Training Services for the Civil Aeronautics Administration, recognizing her efforts in providing qualified pilots for the war effort.

Lt. Willa Brown, Civil Air Patrol

In 1946, Willa Brown ran for Congress, becoming the first African-American woman ever to do so. She failed to get elected, but remained politically active. She used her connections to lobby Congress and the President Truman to desegregate the military, both racially and by gender. On July 26, 1948, Truman signed Executive Order 9981 that eliminated racial separation in the military, starting the process that would ultimately see pilots of all backgrounds flying together.

When the Coffey School closed at the end of the Second World War, Brown set about establishing school aviation programs for children. She went on to be a public school teacher in Chicago, finally retiring at age 65, in 1971. The next year she was appointed to the Federal Aviation Administration's Women's Advisory Board, continuing her legacy of promoting aviation as a career path no matter what a person's background was.

Willa Brown Coffey Chappell passed away in July, 1982, after having a huge impact on aviation and civil rights.

CHAPTER 5 – EMORY MALICK BREAKS THE COLOR BARRIER

Before the spirit of aviation took root in Chicago, there had been few American aviators of color. The group that held the air show in 1931 used as its namesake Bessie Coleman, who got her license to fly in France, as no one in the United States would teach her. One name does pop up, though, and that is Emory Malick.

Malick earned his FAI license in March, 1912. Born December 29, 1881, he grew up in Pennsylvania. He worked as a farm hand after his mother died, and was raised by his father, a carpenter. The 1910 U.S. census shows Malick to be still living in the area, and lists his employment as a carpenter. He worked with his father on the Pennsylvania state capitol building in Harrisburg, and installed wood veneer in railway cars for the Pennsylvania Railroad about that time.

Emory Malick

That his skills were substantial is not to be argued. In 1911 he built his own biplane which, with no formal instruction, he flew on July 24 of that year. Prior to that he had built and flown his own gliders. As others would do later, he sought formal training, and wound up at the Curtiss Aviation School in San Diego, California. He enrolled in January, 1912, and, as noted above, received FAI license #105 in March. This all was nearly lost to history, as the family that wound up with his papers and belongings after his death apparently had no idea that he had any African heritage at all.

We do seem to know this, though. License in hand, he purchased a Curtiss pusher biplane and had it shipped back to Pennsylvania. He flew it over the town of Selinsgrove, "to the wonderment of all", according to the *Selinsgrove Times* newspaper.

From there, he moved to Philadelphia and made a living doing aerial photography for a few companies, giving flying lessons, and the occasional passenger flight. By 1927 Malick had acquired a U.S. Department of Commerce Federal Air Transport License (#1716) as well as a Federal Aircraft Mechanic License (#924). His flying kept his name in the local newspapers, as was common for many aviators of the day.

His most impressive press came after an incident in March, 1928. At a heavily attended airshow, with two passengers on board a Waco biplane, the engine died shortly after takeoff. Seeking to avoid falling into the crowd, he banked and landed the plane in a plowed field, injuring himself and his passengers, as well. The headlines were effusive, such as "Skill and Heroism of Emory C. Malick Prevents Real Tragedy at Camden Yesterday" (*Sunbury Daily Item*). By 1930, it seems that Malick had enough flying, and there is little information about him available after that. He died in Philadelphia in 1958, at the age of 77.

CHAPTER 6 - "THE FIVE BLACKBIRDS" AND THE BESSIE COLEMAN AERO CLUBS

"Irvin Wells was the first to take off, flying a Challenger Commander. The Bill Aikens followed in a Hisso -Eagle Rock. Next was Julian in a Fleet. Then William B. Johnson followed in a Waco 10. Campana followed in a Warner Travellaire. Marie Dickerson took off to great applause in a Kari-Keen. Then Bill followed in a Wright J6 Travellaire. This was a wonderful sight for colored people, just to see seven planes piloted by Negroes in the air at one time."

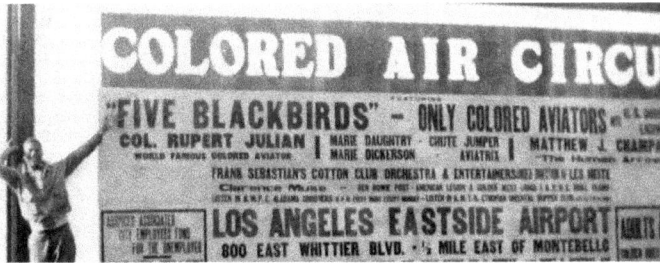

The Bessie Coleman Aero Club 1931 Air Circus

So wrote William J. Powell in his 1934 novel, *Black Wings*. The book is described as a "thinly veiled autobiography" and the passage above accurately reflects the December 6, 1931 air show staged by Powell and "The Colored Air Circus" which flew from Los Angeles' Eastside Airport. Hoping to attract a number of Black aviators, Powell dubbed the group the "Five Blackbirds". It is reported that 40,000 people witnessed the event.

William Jenifer Powell was born in Henderson, Kentucky in 1897. His family moved to Chicago, Illinois when he was a boy and he grew up in middle-class African-American neighborhood. He was accepted to the electrical engineering program at the University of Illinois. Before he graduated, however, the United States was drawn into the First World War, and Powell enlisted. He fought with distinction, reaching the rank of Private First-Class, before being wounded in a poison gas attack on the day the war ended, November 11, 1918.

Powell returned to Chicago and earned his degree in engineering. A natural entrepreneur, Powell bought and ran five automobile service stations on Chicago's South Side, as well as an auto parts store.

In August, 1927, Powell attended an American Legion Convention in Paris, France. He was accompanied by another Legionnaire who was a major in the Illinois National Guard and the pastor of the Berean Baptist Church, in which Powell was a parishioner. They had planned to go to Le Bourget Field, the airport made famous only a few months earlier when Charles Lindbergh landed his Ryan monoplane, dubbed "The Spirit of Saint Louis", after completing the world's first non-stop solo flight across the Atlantic Ocean from Long Island, New York. Aviation interest in both Europe and the United States was reaching a fevered pitch.

Tired from a day spent parading the streets of Paris, the Reverend Major Brannan elected to sit out the trip to the airfield, but Powell found a willing partner in one Burrell Neely, a delegate from Wichita, Kansas. Only acquainted for a few days, Powell found Neely "progressive" and "in for 'most anything".

Anything, it would seem, but taking a ride in an airplane. During the convention, it seemed as though all 30,000 delegates had visited Le Bourget and many had taken flights allowing them to see the Parisian sights from a lofty perspective. Neither man seemed able to muster up the courage to actually go up in an airplane. That was, until they watched a cow being herded up a gangplank into a plane, followed by a couple of crates containing chickens. As the airplane taxied out and took off to deliver its agrarian payload to a stock show across the English Channel in London, the men decided that if women and children and cows and chickens could fly with no ill effects, so could they.

Powell describes his fears as he sat in the passenger plane and the engines warmed up. "Would he land safely? Would he get air-sick as many had told him he would? Would the plane fall? Probably it would be all right going up, but what about coming down? He was sure he would die coming down because he could not stand to come down in a fast elevator – It always seemed as if his stomach was going up to meet his palette." He describes Neely sitting across the aisle from him. "His legs were spread out and he clutched the seat in front to him as though he was bracing himself for a terrible shakeup."

Powell wrote that as terrified as he and Neely were, they were embarrassed by everyone else, including three women and a boy of about seven engaged in casual conversation as the airplane began to taxi and roll out for takeoff. After bumping along the ground for a bit the plane became airborne. As the bumps ceased, both of the Legionnaires got up the courage to open their eyes to discover they were indeed aloft.

They were treated to views of the river Seine, the Eiffel Tower, and even the great cathedral of Notre Dame. Powell marveled at how smooth the flight was, especially as compared to travel on a train. What goes up must come down, however, an as the pilot killed engine power and pointed the nose earthward and the two men went back into fear mode.

It took the motion to stop and the door to open before either would snap out of it.

No air sickness. No harm. Powell decided he had been lied to about the dangers of flight. The two agreed they needed to go up again. They watched for a couple more hours as airplane after airplane departed for destinations around Europe and beyond, filled with travelers who no longer found aviation strange or challenging.

While aviation developed and grew in Europe, especially in France, the United States had yet to adopt the technology as commonplace. In this, Powell saw an opportunity for people of color to reap opportunity in a field fertile for growth.

Powell sought to become a pilot and an aeronautical engineer. In Chicago, this was impossible for him as no flying school would accept a Black candidate. He found the same barrier all over the Midwest, but happened to become acquainted with a school in Los Angeles, California who had no issue teaching anyone who had the will, and the cash.

Hubert Fauntleroy Julian billed himself as "The Black Eagle". Born in Trinidad in 1897, Julian, the son of cocoa plantation manager, attended an excellent private school in Port of Spain. His parents sent him to boarding school in England, but when the Great War broke out in 1914 he traveled to Montreal, Canada. There he took a joyride in an airplane with Billy Bishop, a Canadian World War I flying ace. Bishop gave him flying lessons and he received his Canadian flying license at age 19 and would spend much of the rest of life in pursuits that involved aviation.

In 1921 Julian moved to New York where he married for the first time. He received a patent for "an aviation safety device" he called a "parachuta-gravepreresistra". It involved a pilot controlled blade that would blow open a large umbrella designed to slow the airplane's descent to twenty feet per second. This would seem to be a forerunner to today's aircraft ballistic parachute system. Unable to get the device produced, he sold the patent to a Canadian aircraft company.

Over the course of the next few years, culminating in 1924, Julian hatched a plan to fly a seaplane from the United States, across the Caribbean to Brazil, then across the Atlantic to Liberia. He then intended to fly from there up the coast of Africa and down the Nile to Ethiopia. Julian funded his attempt by selling shares in the trip. The adventure met its end when, while taking off from Flushing Bay in New York the plane became unstable and crashed as one of the pontoons had taken on a considerable amount of water, throwing the plane off the balance.

Julian became the first Black parachutist in 1922 and became quite skilled at it. In one jump, he played the saxophone while descending. In another, he is described as removing his clothes so as to not to get them soaked as a wind shift headed him toward a wet landing off the coast of Atlantic City, New Jersey. Down to his undershorts, the article goes on to say that an unfortunate gust blew those off, also, making him the "world's first nude parachutist".

A parachute performance brought him to the attention of Emperor Haile Selassie of Ethiopia. Selassie was so impressed he granted the aviator Ethiopian citizenship and the rank of "colonel". Julian travelled to Ethiopia and sought establish a commercial airline and shipping line in the country. He went back to the U.S. to recruit Black pilots and technicians for his venture. With little success, he returned to Ethiopia to fly for the emperor. Flying a de Havilland Gypsy Moth, a plane prized by Selassie, he managed to crash and in one swoop reduced the Ethiopian Air Force by a quarter, and got himself expelled from the country.

Julian returned to Ethiopia in 1935 as that country and Italy went to war. He was elevated to Commander of the Royal Ethiopian Air Force. That return trip ended badly again when he was accused of embezzling from the military, and he was ejected once more.

Julian did have a knack for making important and influential friends throughout his life, some more savory than others. In the late 1920's, in spite of fierce popular opposition to Black involvement in aviation in the U.S., Guissepe Bellanca, a noted aircraft designer and manufacturer, gave Julian $3000 to help fund an attempt at a transatlantic solo flight. In 1929 Julian succeeded, making him the first person of color to fly the Atlantic non-stop.

In the 1930's, however, Julian decided to make some fast money flying bootleg whisky from Canada to the East Coast. He quit when he discovered that organized criminals were secreting drugs in the shipments.

In 1931 Julian passed his U. S. pilot's test and received his license.

William Powell met Julian in Chicago on the eve of Powell's leaving for California to earn his pilot's wings. As noted, Powell was determined to bring aviation to the African-American community, and African-Americans to aviation. He saw this a great opportunity to advance in an otherwise hostile business society. He had applied to, and been turned down by, the Army's flight program, and flying schools around the Midwest and East Coast. However, the Warren School of Aeronautics in Los Angeles, California welcomed his application. The school had already trained Chinese, Japanese, Philippine, Mexican and

Indian students, as well as a hundred, or so, white people, and had no misgivings about Powell. For $1000 and a year's study and hard work Powell would emerge a pilot and an aeronautical engineer.

Hubert Julian was in Chicago to pitch his upcoming transatlantic flight and intended to make a parachute jump over the grave of Bessie Coleman in Lincoln Cemetery. Julian asked Powell to fly with him in the plane he had hired to provide the lift. Julian spent the morning at the Pilgrim Baptist Church. The pastor had provided him with $500 toward his ill-fated attempt at an Atlantic crossing years earlier and Julian was there to collect donations to enable his parachute jump on Decoration Day.

Once again, things went awry. In Powell's book he describes Julian as unable to properly fit his parachute, taking so much time that the plane was no longer available for the attempt. Against this backdrop, Julian asked Powell to accompany him on his Atlantic flight as co-pilot and engineer. Powell had yet to learn to fly, but Julian said he would teach him everything he needed to know before the attempt. This required Powell to accompany Julian to New York, leaving on the spot.

William J. Powell

Powell decided that his fortunes would be better served at the Warren School of Aeronautics. Powell owned a Chevrolet that would not be taking the trip west and, so, was for sale. Julian asked to buy the car so he could drive it back to New York. He told Powell he would send him the money as soon as he reached Detroit. Of course, the money never came, so Powell set off with two of the mechanics from his service stations to enroll in aviation classes in L.A.

Powell's goal was to assemble a group of at least ten African-Americans, each trained in flying, navigation, maintenance, and/or aeronautical engineering, as well as the level of business administration it would take to operate a school dedicated to giving Black Americans a springboard into this new industry. There would be several false starts, as his two mechanics, while proficient with automobiles, lacked the reading skills needed to complete the coursework at Warren. However, Powell's networking skills, contacts and hard work finally paid off in the establishment of the Bessie Coleman Aero Clubs, a place where people of color could get the instruction needed to participate in aviation.

Powell had remained in touch with Burrell Neely, and shared his plans to create a beach head for black aviators, technicians, and engineers in the burgeoning aircraft industry. Neely was the business manager for the only African-American newspaper in Kansas, *The Negro Star*. Neely promised Powell that if, or when, Powell finished his aviation education at Warren, Neely would become his business manager. Neely pointed out that for every aviator flying an airplane, there are at least nine other people on the ground making that happen. This venture seemed loaded with potential for lucrative employment among the Black community. The two even talked about building an airline for, and run by, African-

Americans that would serve the South, where people of color were denied the opportunity to fly at all.

At Warren, Powell studied navigation, meteorology, aircraft design, and the Air Traffic Laws published, and enforced, by the U.S. Department of Commerce. He was especially interested in, and good at, the engineering and mathematics surrounding aeronautics. A bright guy, and a quick study, he read and memorized the laws as a final requirement for receiving a physical and his student pilot license. Quizzed by his instructor, he breezed through a review of the regulations. The following day, he went to the office of local air medical examiners. There he easily passed his physical and after plunking down ten dollars, plus a twenty-five cent notary fee, he departed with his student permit.

Powell arrived at Lincoln Airport at least a half hour earlier than the designated time for his first dual instructional flight. His instructor, a Mr. Monteith, arrived on time and ordered that the plane they were going to use be pulled out and warmed up by the mechanics at the field. Powell took the rear cockpit of the dual control Waco 9 biplane, the position that the pilot would occupy in normal circumstances. Monteith sat in the front cockpit and had the same controls available to him that Powell had in the back.

Monteith briefed Powell for his first instructional flight. Monteith would take the plane off from the field and fly it to an altitude of 2000 feet. Instructions were to be conveyed via a "gossport", a speaking tube connected to holes in Powell's flying helmet. When the plane reached altitude, Montieth would hand over control of the stick to Powell. Powell was to move the stick forward or back as required to keep the plane level. "Keep the nose on the horizon".

Nearly as soon as he was handed control, the nose lifted as if hit by a gust or something. Powell pushed the stick forward to pitch the nose down but pushed too far, and the nose dropped well below the horizon. As he pulled back he once again overshot the mark. After several unsuccessful attempts to gain control, Monteith took back the stick and leveled the plane without much effort. "You are too heavy on the stick, just take it easy", Monteith yelled into the gossport to be heard over the engine and wind. Given back control of the plane, Powell was able to make the small adjustments needed to keep the plane level, but it kept him very busy and his attention focused.

After about ten minutes of trying to maintain pitch control, Monteith told Powell he needed to now use the stick to control roll and keep the wings level. For about a half hour Powell worked the controls trying to keep the Waco stable. To complicate matters, the goggles he bought didn't fit properly and air was streaming under the edges, causing his eyes to burn and tears to flow. At some point, he could no longer see to fly the plane and handed control back to his instructor.

Needless to say, the following day Powell bought a properly fit pair of flying goggles. Anxious to go back up, Powell arrived at the field only to find his instructor not there. A call to Monteith revealed the issue, one that pilots to this day suffer with; the base of the clouds was at 500 feet, or so, much too low to fly safely.

Four days of poor weather was followed by a day of mechanical issues keeping the plane from starting. After the best part of a week Powell was chomping at the bit to get back into the air. The same procedure applied to the next flight. Two thousand feet. Controls to Powell. Keep it straight and level. Powell had spent every minute thinking about the first flight, and had apparently figured out what was required to meet the test. Monteith gave Powell control over the rudder pedals, having explained that directional control involved combining the use of the stick to bank the airplane, the rudder pedals to prevent the plane from skidding or slipping through the turn, and need for pitch control as the nose will tend to drop when beginning a turn. Monteith told Powell that he could feel an uncoordinated turn even if wasn't easy to see. If, in a left turn, he could feel a rush of air against his right cheek, he was giving it too much rudder which forced the plane to skid. If he could feel a rush of air on his left cheek he was under-controlling the yaw. Armed with this information, Powell took the controls at 2000 feet.

Monteith pointed out a highway below and told Powell to follow it. After a time, the instructor called for a 180 degree turn to follow the highway back toward the field. After the expected missteps, Powell managed to turn the airplane around and head the other way. He executed a number of 180 degree turns, each smoother than the one before, and the next day ended with 360 degree turns both right and left. Powell had completed six lessons, and had recorded three hours in his logbook.

For lesson seven, Monteith gave Powell control of the throttle. He told Powell that if the engine quit it was important to lower the nose and establish a speed that would keep the plane from stalling. So, in the way flight instructors have done before and forever since, Powell took control and, suddenly, the engine power died. Powell began looking around to see why the engine had quit and, in a few seconds, Monteith yelled for him to get the nose down and reestablish control of the ship. Of course, the sudden lack of power was instructor-induced.

The next time, though, Powell was ready and handled things as he should. He was getting very comfortable controlling the plane and even using landmarks to navigate. After seven hours logged he was making smooth figure eight turns and was able to keep the plane flying smoothly. Anxious to learn to take off and land, Powell asked Monteith when that might happen. Powell had heard of pilots soloing with only five hours logged. Monteith replied that five hours, or seven, were not nearly enough to make a safe pilot. He blamed the high number of airplane accidents on pilots whose training left them unprepared for when something went wrong. Before he could solo, Powell would need to learn to do stalls and stall recovery, side slips, and learn how to get out of spins. Training went from 2000 feet to 5000 feet to leave room for error. Powell executed his first power-off stalls, learning to allow the plane to gain speed and to add power, to recover only after losing a few feet of altitude. On one try, though. Powell felt the plane fall toward the left as the stall was occurring, sending him into a spin. Unsure what to do, he tried pushing the rudder pedals and using the stick to try to level the wings. Monteith took back control and levelled the plane, and spent a great deal of time debriefing Powell on the ground about spin recovery.

Once again, Powell had a day to think about it, and during the next lesson had little trouble exiting three intentional spins with little drama.

After ten hours, Montieth judged Powell ready to start learning take-offs and landings. What would seem like a fairly straightforward venture involved a lot of variables that needed to be learned. A proper preflight check of fuel, oil, the flight surfaces and controls, tires, and everything else involved could prevent failures that at low altitude and speed could turn deadly. Proper engine warm up and running up to full power before trying to take off could keep an engine failure from occurring after the takeoff had commenced. Even the procedures for taxiing the airplane were pretty complicated. Monteith covered everything from a normal takeoff to those things that could go wrong, including overuse of the control stick that could lead to a power on stall, or what happens when operating from high altitude fields where the air might not have enough pressure to support climbing at takeoff speeds.

Powell's first attempt went poorly. The airplane wanted to turn and Powell was unable to keep it going straight. In the early days of aviation, the airfield would be just that. Rather than having a defined runway, or runways, the pilot could point the plane into the wind and use as much as needed of the area to get airborne. As any single-engine propeller pilot can tell you, the spinning blade acts as a gyroscope causing the plane to try to rotate in the opposite direction and, as the plane of the gyroscope changes, as when the nose is raised or lowered, the force works at right angles to the direction of travel, making the plane want to turn. Without a good feel for rudder pedals, Powell wound up over controlling and was unable to maintain a straight line.

Once again, a sense of failure was followed by a good night's rest and time to think about what had gone wrong. The next day Powell adjusted his feet on the rudder pedals so that he was only using toe pressure, and took off straight as an arrow.

Landings should have been more complicated, but Powell had practiced power off, spiraling descents and was getting very good at putting the ship down without drama. Having figured out how to get successfully off the ground, he performed four landings and takeoffs in quick succession. On the next landing, Monteith instructed Powell to taxi to end of the field and stop. Montieth got out of the plane and checked the elevator trim and Powell's seat belt, and told him to take off, circle the field at 1000 feet, and then land the airplane. Powel was about to solo, with thirteen hours logged as a student.

For his first attempt it seemed as though Powell spent more time paying attention to the people on ground who had come out of their offices and hangars to watch. He began his landing approach much too high to pull it off, even slipping off altitude and using every other trick that he had learned. At least he had the sense not to force the landing and added power and went around the pattern once again. The next attempt Powell came in too low and, once again, had to give it power and go around. His third approach, though, was perfect, resulting in a three-point landing right on the paved circle that was the center of the airfield.

Ten hours of instruction later, Powell found himself at Mines Field, where he took a written exam of Air Commerce Regulations and Air Traffic Laws. Easily passed, his flight test involved a number of landings and maneuvers, all of which Powell had prepared for. He was now a licensed private pilot.

Having accomplished his first goal, Powell set about to try to interest investors and potential board members in forming the Bessie Coleman Aero Clubs. Five months before Powell would graduate with his pilot's license and a degree in aeronautical engineering, his friend and soon-to-be business manager, Burrell Neely, arrived in Los Angeles ready to take on the job of raising funds and personnel. Articles of incorporation were drawn up and the club became a reality, at least on paper.

A letter, written to the Commerce Department by Neely, asked for recommendations they might have for any Black aviators and aircraft mechanics. The November 6, 1929, response states that the department "...was not aware of any negro who holds a commercial pilot's license, or a mechanic's license." It went on to say, though, "There is, of course, nothing in the Air Commerce Regulations that would prohibit the holding of such a license."

Neely and Powell decided that the letter should be published in African-American newspapers, proving that this was a wide open opportunity that should be seized. This resulted in a great deal of interest, including from one James Herman Banning, of Ames, Iowa, who, in fact, held a commercial pilot's license. Banning would, along with Thomas C. Allen, fly from coast to coast in September and October, 1932. Dr. A. Porter Davis, known in Kansas as "The Flying Physician" also sought to join the endeavor.

Slowly, with many missteps, the Bessie Coleman Aero Clubs became a reality. Initially its board consisted of people from the Los Angeles area who had either the aviation skills to take a role in the flight operations, or the management wherewithal, and the financial investment, to become part of the executive group.

Neely and Powell reckoned that with the positive response to the letter and articles covering the club, they would take the show on the road and try to raise more capital, all while getting more people involved from across the country. In order to finance the enterprise, the group took advantage of a visit to Los Angeles by a man who was then the only Black member of Congress, Oscar De Priest, a representative from Chicago. When De Priest arrived by train, Banning and Powell flew an airplane over the station and then, flying "S" turns and circles so as not to get ahead of it, led the motorcade with the congressman to his hotel. They arranged for De Priest to attend a ceremony the next day where the club's airplane would be christened the "Oscar De Priest" at Lincoln Airport. The finale was that De Priest would ride in the plane with Banning, making it the first time that he, or any politician, had flown with a Black aviator.

The attention drawn to the club by the event allowed them to purchase a new Ford Model A sedan and prepare a fundraising tour through Black communities across the country. On the car was lettered with "Bessie Coleman Aero Clubs Tour of 100 Cities" and the silhouette of an airplane.

While Burrell Neely and Ed Graham toured the country, Banning and Powell used the Eagle airplane they owned to do pilot and navigator training with people who were to be the charter membership, and would go on to teach the skills they had learned to other aspiring African-American pilots and mechanics.

Over the next few months, however, the driving tour was foundering. While they received warm welcomes in a number of cities, from Phoenix to New Orleans to Chicago, little investment was forthcoming. The usual reason given was that the idea of Black aviators was so farfetched that it seemed impractical. They were told that, had they arrived by plane instead of by Ford, that the response might have been different. Things got even more difficult in Wichita, Kansas, when a check they were given as a donation bounced after Neely cashed it a drug store. This led to the seizure of the Ford, a problem solved only after several days, and the intervention and $100 redemption fee, of a local mechanic named Thomas C. Allen. In return, Allen wanted to be part of the Operations Group of the club.

The plane, for which the club had paid $3500, was kept at Lincoln Airport, and brought out every morning, whether to flown or not, to run up the engine in order to keep it mechanically sound. On one such morning, with the club's chief mechanic William Browne unable to get to the field early enough to prepare the lane for a training flight, a friend of his, an aspiring aviator, but with no real training or experience, agreed to pull the plane out and do the warmup. Finding himself alone with the plane, with some time before it was scheduled to fly, Sydney Walker decided he would take the ship up for a quick trip around the airport. Witnesses said that "...the ship was seen to zigzag down the field, suddenly rise up from the ground about twenty-five feet, then shoot straight down like a bullet, crashing into the ground and catching fire." While Walker was apparently unhurt, the uninsured airplane was demolished.

About that time the club received a letter from the Mississippi State Fair offering an appearance fee of $2500. Neely and Powell worked quickly to purchase a Kinner Crown airplane secured by a $1000 down payment and one of the rent houses owned by Mrs. Susie Hancock, the lady who got to christen the "Oscar De Priest", and who was now a member of the board.

The trip to Mississippi got underway poorly, and turned for the worst from there. Unable to raise funds for two people to drive to the fair while Powell and Banning flew, the road trip was called off. Neely, feeling a sense of failure and despair over his ability to raise funds, resigned from the group. Finally, a misstep in navigation put Banning and Powell on a beach on the east coast of Baja California, Mexico, out of fuel and thoroughly lost. In trying to navigate using familiar landmarks, while flying much higher than they generally would, Powell failed to locate El Centro, California, south of the Salton Sea. Instead, they saw a body of water with the same general shape to their south and thought that their compass must be misbehaving. In fact, the body of water was the Laguna Salada, Baja California's smaller salt water lake. So, turning to look for El Centro to the south of the water they flew hundreds of miles off course.

At some point the airplane ran low on fuel and the aviators realized it was time to find a soft spot to put it down. The found a stretch of sandy beach where Powell executed an uneventful landing. Thinking they had landed on the Pacific coast, they began walking with the sea to their left, which would have been north, toward civilization. After about four hour's journey, finding nothing, Powell had a revelation. Taking a stick and putting in the sand, he marked the position of the Sun's shadow. He waited a few minutes and marked the position again. It was then that he realized that there was nothing wrong with the airplane's compass. They were on the east coast of the Baja California peninsula, on the Gulf of California. Any help would lie in the other direction.

After a couple of days trying to locate civilization on foot, they saw lights in the distance at night and found themselves in the village of San Filipe. To their amazement, they encountered an ex-patriate American who ran the local grocery. Pleased to find someone with whom to speak English, the shopkeeper fed them and arranged for transportation to refuel their plane. This allowed them to fly north and reenter the U.S. through Yuma, Arizona. After the expected discussions with the Customs Department, the flyers went on to Phoenix. Having missed the Mississippi objective, the decided to perform impromptu air shows there, and raise the money required to pay off the plane.

They nearly had the plane seized. A Los Angeles newspaperman, Oliver Betts, with whom the club had parted company over advertising costs, planted a rumor that the pilots were absconding with the Crown and had no intention of returning to L.A. This put at risk Powell's down payment and Mrs. Hancock's rent house. Banning returned to California, putting the rumors to rest, but serious damage had been done by newspaper articles circulated by Betts. Formerly interested parties elected not to invest.

With the plane already half way there, it was decided that a barnstorming tour of Texas might bring in needed capital. While that was being discussed in California, Powell and Banning received a visit from a couple of white gentlemen whom they took to be detectives. In fact, the men offered the pilots $250 per head to smuggle Chinese immigrants across the border from Mexico. While seeming to be the answer to their cash problems, both pilots agreed that it was not worth the personal risk, or the damage it could do to the reputation of Bessie Coleman Aero Clubs.

The barnstorming tour was, likewise, unsuccessful. The Betts letter had preceded them and they found no interest in investing. To make matters worse, on the trip home, Banning failed to get airborne from a very small field near Jacksonville, Texas, and, with the engine dead, put the plane nose down into a chicken house while avoiding a crash into a line of cars filled with spectators.

Irvin Wells, one of the board members had enough cash to purchase another airplane back in Los Angeles. Not to be defeated, plans were laid to hold "The First All-Negro Air Show" at Lincoln Field. Powell continued to train pilots and on Labor Day, 1931, the Goodyear Blimp dropped a wreath of flowers to honor Bessie Coleman, and pilots Herman Banning, William Aikens, Matthew Campana, Maxwell Love, and Lottie Theodore flew exhibitions. 15,000 people showed up for the event.

Buoyed by their success, Powell, Wells and Aikens became the "first Negro Formation Flying Group in America". Love and Theodore had learned parachuting and were becoming quite good at it, and Campana was, likewise, building aerobatic skills.

Word of the air show success got around quickly, which prompted Hubert Julian, fresh from his adventures in Ethiopia, to rejoin the group. The addition of "The Black Eagle of Harlem" served to build another level of excitement as plans were laid for another air show, this one to benefit the Associated City Employees Fund for the Unemployed of Los Angeles. Which brings us back to December 6, 1931 and Eastside Airport.

Marie Dickerson, introduced in the preceding chapter, was an African-American actress and singer who was part of the initial investors in the Bessie Coleman Aero Clubs. She was taught to fly by Powell and Banning, and had shown a real knack for navigation.

Ms. Dickerson was to be part of the hoopla surrounding the great air show. She and Hubert Julian were to meet the mayor of Los Angeles on the steps of city hall. Dressed in flying togs, Julian and Dickerson posed with Mayor John C. Porter, City Councilman John R. Quinn, Sheriff Eugene Biscailuz, and a group made up from the Bowie Post of the American Legion, and the Los Angeles Police Band. The entire ceremony was broadcast on KECA radio, a mainstream station that would, eventually, become the ABC affiliate in Southern California. This marked the first time in history that any African-American had been greeted on the Los Angeles city hall steps.

On the day of the air show, "Colonel" Julian was to preform aerobatics and a triple parachute jump. As seemed to be the norm, he managed a single parachute jump and declared himself too tired from the experience to perform his aerobatic show. As past experiences showed, he was a lot more talk than action. When the flight of seven pilots and planes flew later in the day. Six of them landed a Vail Airfield a few miles away. Julian never showed up. He apparently flew to the wrong airport and waited for the others to arrive.

That left Powell, Banning, Aikens, Johnson, and Wells to return to Grand Central, with Marie Dickerson flying the slot position between the wings of the "V" formation. Arriving back at the airfield, the group flew in the "V" and in echelon, with the airplanes arranged diagonally, and trailing one another. Each pilot, in turn, "did his or her special stunt", to the roar of the crowd. Maxwell Love and Marie Daugherty performed parachute jumps. In spite of the absence of the top-billed "Black Eagle of Harlem", the show was great success.

To cap the festivities, Frank Sebastian's Cotton Club Entertainers performed. The club was located in Culver City, California, and, like the original Cotton Club in Harlem, New York, featured Black musicians, singers and dancers. In fact, Marie Dickerson was a frequent headliner there. It had valet parking and three dance floors. Notables including Louis Armstrong played there. Culver City was the home of the Hal Roach, RKO, and Metro-Goldwyn-Mayer movie studios, so the Cotton Club had a readymade audience of celebrities. Like its (unrelated) namesake in New York, the entertainment was Black, but the clientele was all white. Needless to say, with that caliber of musical entertainment a good time was had by all.

While Oliver Betts once again snubbed the group, the success of the endeavor got picked up by a journalist from the *Pittsburgh Courier*, resulting in it being reprinted in African-American newspapers across the country. The group felt it was time for a long-distance, perhaps coast-to-coast, flight performed by Black aviators.

Hubert Julian, once again, imposed himself. He had put a large down payment of $30,000 on a Bellanca airplane that was hangared in New York. This was plane in which he intended to make a transatlantic flight. He failed to pay off the balance, however, and lost his considerable investment. In California he sought to buy a Lockheed plane under the auspices of the club, but the group decided that he acted without their consultation and on a plane that was already an obsolete model. Then, he held a christening for his purchase at a ceremony that included members of the American Legion. The money raised was not sufficient to pay for the airplane but Julian signed a 60-day note for the balance. Once, again, he failed to raise the money and lost his plane.

He convinced a local woman, a young widow named Reversta Tellis, to pay $500 down on another plane. Christened the "Reversta Tolerance" the airplane never made the transcontinental trip as, again, the needed funds failed to materialize.

Frustrated with the failures, and beginning to fade heat for Julian's unkept promises, Powell and the Aero Club began to make other plans. They knew that making a long-distance flight would solidify their credibility. It was suggested, and then decided, that the group would enter the National Air Races to be held starting on August 27, 1932.

While most of the fifty-six planes entered in the Pacific Wing of the race were state of the art and high performance, all the club had to use was the plane they used for training, a Lincoln-Paige biplane. It was powered by a Curtis OX-5, a water-cooled V-8 engine renowned for its reliability, having been the staple powerplant for venerated Curtiss JN-4 "Jenny". That decided, the engine was tuned up and airframe inspected and checked in preparation for a cross-country flight.

Powell qualified the Lincoln-Paige at Mines Field at an average speed of 94.7 miles per hour. While not a great speed, it was enough to get them into the race.

At the same time, but unbeknownst to Powell, Banning and John Hensley decided to prepare another plane and set out to fly from Los Angeles to New York. They reasoned that since they didn't have to stop and checkpoints along the way, they could beat Powell to the goal and become the first African-Americans to complete a transcontinental flight.

While this unwanted competition angered many members of the group, Powell decided that the idea of competing teams of Black flyers would add publicity to the already unique idea of Air Derby participants of color. Two days after qualifying, Powell flew to Mines Field for takeoff on the first leg of the L.A. to Cleveland, Ohio race. The first checkpoint was Yuma, Arizona. So, two by two, the contestants departed the field, cheered on by a huge crowd, almost exclusively white.

In Yuma Powell was surprised and delighted to find out that he was not trailing everyone as he had expected. The plane had been rigged ("trimmed", in modern parlance) for speed rather than climb performance. Powell headed the airplane toward the San Gorgonio pass in order to get through the first barrier of mountains *en route*. Climbing gently to 3,000 feet the plane easily cleared the mountains and the altitude provided relief from the desert temperatures at ground level below him as he passed by Palm Springs and on toward Yuma. Upon sighting Yuma he put the plane into a gentle dive. The speed gained on descent put Wells and him ahead of a couple of competitors that were flying level at about 500 above the ground. They passed the white finish line tape ahead of both, and landed to join the rest of racers.

Before the next leg to Tucson, the pair discovered a broken fuel line. This cost them a half hour, or so, before they could affect the repair and get underway. As they picked their way through low spots in the terrain through the Mohawk Mountains they started getting an engine miss, thought to be caused by a stuck valve. Before they could reach Tucson the vibration became bad enough to warrant a forced landing, but with wide open desert below them, that was accomplished with little trouble.

Having replaced the offending broken valve spring, they took off again for Tucson. Arriving in Tucson the next leg would be flagged off in 45 minutes with the destination El Paso, Texas. Instead, the pair again dealt with a poorly running engine as a brass carburetor float, a device that controls the amount of gas that goes into the engine, had cracked, and had filled with gasoline. With no repair facilities on the field, two hours passed while they went into town and found someone who could solder and repair the part.

Leaving Tucson late they needed to climb to 7,000 feet to clear the Dos Cabezas Mountains. Their chances of reaching El Paso before dark were getting slim. To make matters worse they had to fly between two desert thunderstorms, while just following the narrow crack of sunlight they could see ahead.

As aircraft were not allowed to fly without navigation lighting between one half hour before sunrise and one-half hour after sunset the flyers began looking for a place to land to keep from violating the law and begin disqualified. They plotted a course to Mt. Riley, New Mexico. At sunset the Mt. Riley airport turned on its rotating beacon and the intrepid fliers set down the airplane for the night. Upon landing the plane was overheating and steam was coming from the radiator. An inspection resulted in finding two hose clamps that had come loose. With no replacements the flyers wrapped the connections in tape and decided to try for El Paso in the morning.

Only forty miles from El Paso, but miles from any other town, they spent the night in the plane. Early in the morning they took off and landed in El Paso at about 8 o'clock. Two new radiator hoses and an oil change later, they started the airplane only to find it lacked power. They departed for Roswell, New Mexico about five in the afternoon, after checking and adjusting nearly everything on the engine, but now, with full power.

Climbing over the Sacramento Mountains about an hour out of El Paso, the engine began to overheat again. It then began losing power. As the revolutions per minute dropped, it became obvious that the plane would not sustain flight and had to be set down in what could only be considered rough terrain. Powell turned the nose upwind and killed the power, gliding down looking for a solution. "At the last moment, he pulled back the stick and set the plane on a little knoll." Momentum carried the plane forward and it struck a rock, nosed over the edge of the hill, and landed upside down. Fearing fire, the pilots scrambled clear, but escaped without a scratch.

Powell and Wells, now about seventy five miles from El Paso, recollected seeing a ranch house in the area as they flew over. They took off in the rugged hills in the direction that they believed the farmhouse to be. As night fell, Powell recalled finding help in Baja California after dark by following the light from local houses. They found a suitable vantage point and looked for lights. Spotting the house, it took them until two thirty in the morning to reach the ranch, which woke the dogs in residence. Knowing that they had reached a place that someone lived, in spite of the lights now being extinguished, the pilots found a spot to sleep until morning.

The ranch hand that found them in the morning was also a Texas Ranger, and, obviously, surprised to be in the presence of two Black men in flying attire. They told the Texan what happened, but the refused to believe that anyone could put a plane down in the mountains and survive. And then, to quote Powell, the conversation got more troubling. "I never heard of a n***** flyer, anyway, and furthermore I believe youse (*sic*) are the two fellers that killed a milkman in El Paso night before last and that you are trying to disguise yourselves in flying suits."

The pilots produced their licenses, which had pictures of them, which satisfied the ranch hand, at least temporarily. Shortly after, however, a car full of armed white men drove up to ranch. While this looked bad for the flyers, it turned out the driver, the ranch owner's son, was a pilot and had seen the two in El Paso. This led to a lot of what could today be called hangar flying. It turned out that the rifles were out because the men had been hunting. The rancher's son convinced the others that, after a good breakfast, they should go try to locate the airplane.

The ranch owner, one Gibson MacGregor, owned 350,000 acres of land as one of the richest cattle barons in Texas at the time. His son, the pilot who was named Douglas, the flyers, and another couple of the hunting party, drove as far as they could in their car, and then located the plane on foot. With lots of resources at this disposal, McGregor had the plane disassembled and brought to the ranch, but only after photographing the ship on its back, reasonably unharmed.

The El Paso daily papers ran the story, making the pilots instant local celebrities, especially among the Black community. With the plane left in the care of a local mechanic, Powell and Wells returned to Los Angeles. In the meantime, Banning and Hensley had obtained the use of an airplane they thought would be suitable for a transcontinental trip.

James Herman Banning was born in Oklahoma in 1900 and, after high school, spent two years studying engineering at Iowa State

University. Becoming interested in aviation, he tried, as had Powell, to find an instructor in the Midwest that would take on an African-American student. As Powell discovered, this proved to be futile through the established flight training schools. After being rejected in a number of cities, he returned to Iowa where he found an Army officer willing to train him and, in 1926, when the U.S. Department of Commerce began issuing pilot licenses, Banning found himself as the only African-American in the country with a U.S. license.

The airplane that Banning and Hensley acquired was an Eagle Rock with a Curtiss OXX-6 engine. This engine was an improvement on the OX-5 like the one that Powell and Wells used for their ill-fated air race attempt. It featured dual magnetos, giving added reliability should one fail, and another 10 horsepower (100, versus the 90 generated by the OX-5).

The plane belonged to a certain Arthur Dennis, who had purchased the plane for his own use, but had never reached the point that he could fly it solo. Dennis was a member of the so-called "sporting class" in the Black community of the time. He went by the name "Small Black". Powell wrote, "...he represents the first class of Negroes who will offer a potential market for airplanes – the sporting class who always manage to purchase just about what they want."

Dennis got the local community to provide an additional four or five hundred dollars to purchase new magnetos, cylinder heads, a propeller and a compass for the Eagle Rock in order to make it reliable for a long trip.

By the eve of his transcontinental flight, Banning had around 800 hours of flying time, 400 of those with the Bessie Coleman Aero Clubs.

He held only a private pilot license, very likely because the opportunity for people of color to qualify for an air transport pilot (commercial) license was quite difficult, or, at least, that was the contention. Some other Black pilots managed to get their ATP certification, but facilities to do so were seriously limited.

Dennis had prevented Banning and Hensley from leaving Los Angeles while the air race was taking place, as he hoped that the Aero Clubs pilots in the race might make it across the country. The plan had been that, having reached the end of the race in Cleveland, Powell and Wells would fly on to New York. When Powell and Wells ended their air race in Texas, it was apparent that they would not become the first Black coast-to-coast flyers. At that point "Small Black" gave the go ahead for the attempt.

Dennis had supplied plane and the money to upgrade and refurbish it, but would not give the operating funds needed for the fuel, oil and other expenses for the flight. By this time both Banning and Hensley had exhausted their funds, so the flight hinged on finding additional investment. The source became one Thomas C. Allen.

Thomas Cox Allen was born, and lived in, Quitman Texas. He is quoted as saying, "I got the flying bug when I was a young boy in East Texas. We had a farm with about 50 acres of grass and one day an airplane made a forced landing. I'd never seen an airplane on the ground before." The pilots offered to pay someone to watch the airplane, saying that airplanes attracted cattle "...like a salt block." Planes left in pastures were prone to being eaten by the bovines. When the pilots were leaving, Allen said to one of them, "I'm going to fly an airplane someday." The pilot replied, "You just keep that in your mind and someday you will."

Allen's mother was a teacher, and moved the family to Oklahoma City for a position there. Allen, for years after school and whenever he could, rode his bike to the local airfield and "...just hung around". He asked the proprietor what it would take for him to learn to fly. A deal was struck for $300, which involved swapping a saxophone worth $100, and working off the rest.

After several lessons over many months Allen was likely ready to solo, but was unable to as a $500 surety bond was required. His fortunes changed when he was seventeen, and the instructor was away from the field. It is recounted that some airfield employees got drunk on home brew liquor and dared Allen to fly the plane, which he did successfully. The plane's owner saw his ship in the air and surmised what had transpired and returned to the airfield "...in a rage." However, "...the others were telling him, if he could teach (Allen) to fly, he could teach anyone. So he billed himself that way – 'If I could teach a Negro boy to fly then I could teach you'". Apparently, his business boomed after that.

Allen worked at numerous jobs as an aircraft mechanic in Texas and Kansas, including for the infant Braniff Airline. He had an on again, off again relationship with the Bessie Coleman Aero Clubs and Herman Banning, but enough money for the fuel and oil for the first leg of the trip, and the mechanical skills that would likely be required to complete the trip. Their intent was to raise money at each stop to pay for the next leg. Ultimately, the flight would take three weeks with less than two days actually in the air.

On September 18, 1932, Banning and Allen, now calling themselves "The Flying Hobos" left Los Angeles with less than $100 between them. Banning would later say he "had $25 and a dream". On

October 9, they landed their Eagle Rock at Curtiss Airport in Valley Stream, Long Island, New York.

FIRST TRANS-CONTINENTAL FLIGHT
Los Angeles to New York
October 9th 1932. Flying Time 41 hrs. 27 min.

Allen and Banning – "The Flying Hobos"

What followed was a plan to exhibit the plane and the flyers nationally. A donor so taken by the feat arranged a new Curtiss radial engine for the plane, bringing its performance up to date. Things went south, however when the plane was forced down, out of fuel, due to headwinds that left them short of their destination while flying out of Pittsburgh, Pennsylvania. The wing was damaged badly and the repairs amounted to $500. An appeal to the Black community failed to raise the necessary funds, so the plane remained in Pittsburgh under a mechanics lien and the "Flying Hobos" returned to Los Angeles by bus.

The friction between Banning and Powell dated back to the December, 1931 airshow where Hubert Julian got top billing, angering Banning. It was especially irksome that when, after all of the hype, Julian failed to deliver.

Being managed by John Hensley, Banning and Allen booked exhibitions in Southern California beginning with one at Eastside Airport in Los Angeles. The following weekend they were booked in San Diego, but, in the meantime, Thomas Allen elected to go it alone, leaving Banning without a partner. Banning approached Powell, and, after apologies and reconciliation, they agreed that the common goal of bringing African-Americans into aviation was most important and made plans for the weekend's flying,

The exhibition was postponed by rain for one, then two, then three consecutive Sundays. Powell was unable to perform on February 5, 1933, as he had a previous commitment to his church. Banning set out on his own to San Diego.

Banning's plane was being readied at Lindbergh Field. A white Navy pilot volunteered to fly Banning over the air show site, Camp Kearney Field. The airplane they were in was not a dual control plane, the pilot in the rear cockpit, Banning as a passenger in the front. Arriving at Camp Kearney they found a good sized crowd, and, apparently, the young Naval Aviator wanted to show Banning and the crowd that he, too, had flying skills. Putting in full power, he pulled the plane into a steep climb, which resulted in a power-on stall and spin much too close to ground to recover, or to use a parachute. Banning was killed instantly on contact.

The Bessie Coleman Aero Club

Over the next couple of years the Bessie Coleman Aero Club and later a group called Black Wings, endeavored to promote aviation in the Black community. They attracted considerable excitement and support with a play called "Ethiopia Spreads Her Wings", a tale about a family whose home and livelihood was saved by an involvement in the still growing field of aviation. The Aero Clubs disbanded in 1934, a victim of The Great Depression, as did Black Wings not long after.

Sadly, William Jenifer Powell died in 1942, likely due to respiratory damage dating to his service in France in World War I, his dreams unfulfilled and crushed by the economic collapse and the entrenched racism in the United States. It would several more decades to see his intentions met, at least in a small way, but still not as he wanted, with people of color as the vanguard of the industry.

CHAPTER 7 - THE ROAD TO TUSKEGEE

In a previous chapter some of the women involved in the Challenger Air Pilots' Association were covered, and some mention was made of the men who were involved in the group's founding and success. The association was formed in Chicago in 1931 by, and for, African-American aviators with the goal of making flying available to people of color as widely as it was already by then to white pilots.

John C. Robinson and Cornelius Coffey were auto mechanics in Detroit, Michigan when Bessie Coleman met her death in a flying accident in 1926. Coleman had a dream of opening a flight school for people of color, and Robinson and Coffey were inspired to finish her work. The two attempted to enroll at the Curtiss-Wright Aeronautical University in Chicago, but were denied. Coffey, in conjunction with his employer, filed suit for racial discrimination. Robinson took a job at the school as a janitor so as to gain as much knowledge as he could by observing and auditing classes.

Apparently, as he was cleaning up, Robinson found an aviation magazine in the school's trash that had an advertisement for a Heath Parasol airplane kit, available less engine, for three hundred dollars. He and Coffey purchased the kit, and, with the help of other auto mechanics working in loaned storefront space at a South Side Chicago garage, built the plane. Lacking a proper airplane motor, they adapted one from Coffey's motorcycle.

Robinson and Coffey had been befriended by one of the instructors at the Curtiss-Wright School, who volunteered to evaluate the airplane. At Washington Park in Chicago, he did taxi tests on the grass field to see whether the plane would break anything or shake itself apart. Satisfied that the aircraft was well built, the instructor took off, flew, and landed, and declared the airplane to be easily flyable.

Impressed, the school's management rethought their "whites only" stand, and offered Robinson and Coffey evening instruction as a segregated class of two. They accepted, and Coffey dropped his suit. The school further offered that the pair could teach other students of color after they successfully completed their own courses.

Coffey and Robinson graduated and began teaching aeronautics courses to African-Americans. Their first group comprised mechanics from Robinson's South Side garage, as well as Janet Harmon Bragg. The working relationship with the otherwise all-white school staff became too uncomfortable for the pair after a time, which prompted them to establish their own aeronautics school. Thus, in 1931, the Challenger Air Pilots' Association was formed.

The city of Chicago refused to allow the establishment of a Blacks-only airport which led the Challenger pilots to Robbins, then a predominately African-American town south of Chicago. Seeing an opportunity, Mayor Samuel Nichols approved of, and encouraged the venture. The group, with substantial help from volunteers, cleared trees and rocks to create a single runway, and built a hangar large enough for the one airplane that the club owned, mainly from scrap or salvaged lumber.

The Challenger Air Pilots Association at Robbins Field

For a couple of years they trained African-American aviators at the Robbins site, but in late 1933 a snowstorm leveled the hangar, and it was never rebuilt. This led to a diaspora of Challenger pilots that would, eventually, come back in focus with the establishment of the Tuskegee Airmen.

John C. Robinson was originally from Florida, born in November, 1903. He grew up in Gulfport, Mississippi, and that is where he got to see a barnstormer in a float plane in operation and his interest in aviation was born. Taking classes in high school in mechanics and machinery, he started down the road that would result in his career as a mechanic. Mississippi would not permit people of African descent to attend school past tenth grade, so Robinson applied to the Tuskegee Institute in Alabama. He graduated three years later having studied auto mechanics, and getting a solid grounding in math, literature, history and composition.

Even with a degree in automobile mechanics, Robinson was hard pressed to find a mechanic job in Gulfport, as the local businesses were owned by whites. He took his degree and skills to Detroit, reasoning that automotive jobs should be more plentiful there, but only managed to find work as a mechanic's assistant, at least to begin with. In many cases his extensive knowledge posed a threat to his white coworkers. Eventually, though, he was promoted to mechanic with a commensurate raise in pay.

Things seemed to be getting even rosier when we was approached by a taxicab company, with a mechanic's job that doubled his income. He eventually decided to go elsewhere, as, during the age of liquor prohibition, being in a city that bordered Canada, his employers were running bootleg whiskey.

He wound up at a small airfield at some point, and performed repairs on the engine of a Curtiss "Jenny", earning him a ride in a Waco biplane. This experience gave him even more of a drive to learn to fly, which pointed him to the Curtiss-Wright school in Chicago.

With a thriving African-American community on the South Side of Chicago, Robinson was able to open his own automotive garage, leading to the events described above.

Cornelius Robinson Coffey was born in Newport, Arkansas on September 26, 1903. His father, a railroad worker moved them to Omaha, Nebraska when he was a teenager, and it was there that he took his first flight in an airplane at age thirteen. Once bitten, the flying bug became a full blown obsession. At sixteen he moved to Chicago and made a living repairing automobiles and motorcycles and it was during this period that

Coffey and John Robinson became friends. In 1925 Coffey enrolled in an automotive trade school in Chicago, and worked with Robinson at a garage owned by white Chevrolet dealer, Emil Mack.

Mack supported both Coffey's and Robinson's application to Curtiss-Wright and paid their tuition. The school only turned them away when they appeared in the flesh and the school's management discovered they were Black men. In fact, Mack was the force behind the lawsuit that was brought against the school, and as noted previously, the school relented.

After the airfield in Robbins was abandoned, Coffey went on to get his commercial license in August, 1938. With that, he opened his own Cornelius Coffey School of Aeronautics at Harlem Airport in Chicago. It was there that the first, of only two, federally funded Civilian Pilot Training Program (CPTP) flight schools for aviators of color was established.

John C. Robinson returned to Tuskegee, Alabama in May, 1933, after the Robbins era, and lobbied his alma mater to support an aviation program for African-Americans. The school did so, and established an aviation program. In 1939, Tuskegee became the second CPTP.

Meanwhile, with conflict brewing in North Africa involving the Kingdom of Ethiopia, Africa's only independent Black nation, and the Italian military. Emperor Haile Selassie sent out a call for aviation experts and technicians to assist his fledgling air force program. Robinson responded to the cause in May, 1935. Though several westerners responded and were assisting in building the operation, Robinson was the first person of African descent, a fact that fit well with Selassie's vision of an all-Black Imperial Ethiopian Air Force.

After only a few months there, training flyers and technicians, mostly by using an interpreter to get around the language barrier, Robinson was promoted to the rank of colonel and put in charge of the Air Force. Robinson is credited with training seventy new pilots and getting the fleet of aircraft doubled for a total of twenty-four.

All of Ethiopia's aircraft were observation or training planes. Robinson had some of the planes modified so that bombs could be dropped. They were about to face a modern, well-armed Italian military, with one of the largest air forces in Europe, bent on occupation.

On October 3, 1935, Mussolini's forces attacked Adowa, Ethiopia and bombed it into submission.

Robinson continued his efforts, flying reconnaissance missions, carrying Selassie to the front to observe, and even engaging in aerial combat, earning him the nickname, "The Brown Condor of Ethiopia".

The Ethiopian forces were no match for Italy's modern mechanized army, and fell in 1936. Robinson returned to Chicago and resumed teaching and flying. His efforts in Ethiopia made the American news media and became the nexus around efforts to include African-Americans in military aviation, leading to his other appellation, "The Father of the Tuskegee Airmen".

Cornelius Coffey, in the meantime, remained in Chicago at Harlem Airport, teaching and promoting aviation. It is estimated that he trained over 1,500 aviators at his school, including the woman who would ultimately become his wife and business partner, Willa Brown.

The Coffey School of Aeronautics

Charles Alfred Anderson was born in Bryn Mawr, Pennsylvania in 1907. He developed an interest in aviation as a youth and by age twenty he had saved enough money for flying lessons, but couldn't find anyone willing to take on a Black flight student. After managing to get into a ground school, and hang around the airport picking up information, his unique solution was to pool his money with loans from friends and family and purchase his own airplane.

He bought a Velie Monocoupe, a high-wing monoplane with an enclosed cabin, designed by Don Luscombe, a pioneer in aviation design and manufacture. He would start up and taxi his plane around the field, giving it increased power, until he learned to get it airborne and back on the ground successfully. Pilots of tailwheel airplanes know that this is no mean feat for the uninitiated.

As he owned an airplane he was allowed into a local flying club. One of the members, Russell Thaw, was a licensed pilot but did not have his own airplane. Thaw did, however, have a mother in Atlantic City, New Jersey. Anderson and Thaw struck a deal by which Thaw would rent and pilot Anderson's Monocoupe, while Anderson accompanied him and built up logbook hours and experience to his goal of ultimately getting his own pilot license in 1929.

Anderson went on to get his air transport pilot license in 1932, under the tutelage of Ernest H. Buehl, a German immigrant and former fighter pilot. Buehl came to the United States to begin charting and opening up transcontinental air mail routes, and over his career would open three airports, the first in 1928 in Bucks County, Pennsylvania. When a white examiner refused to issue an ATP license to Anderson, Buehl intervened, and Anderson became the first African-American to hold a commercial pilot license.

Dr. Albert Forsythe met Anderson sometime around 1933. Forsythe was born in Nassau in the Bahamas, and came to the United States in his teens to study architecture at the Tuskegee Institute. He also attended the University of Illinois, received his bachelor's degree from the University of Toledo in Ohio, and went on get a dental degree from McGill University in Canada.

Forsythe and Anderson both felt strongly about the need to create opportunities for Black men to become aviators. They determined that getting the public's attention would help motivate their cause and, in 1933 the pair flew a single engine, high wing, Fairchild 24, christened "The Pride of Atlantic City" on a round trip from New Jersey to Los Angeles, and back. They were the first African-American pilots to do a coast-to-coast round trip, which made news and did, in fact, further their goals.

In 1934 the pair followed up by flying a Monocoupe christened "The Booker T. Washington" on what was billed as a South American Goodwill Tour. Their intent was to visit several Caribbean Islands and fly on to South America. The flight ended when departing Trinidad, they hit turbulence and landed hard, damaging the airplane and slightly injuring

Anderson. They returned to the U.S. on a commercial flight, but the trip generated more news coverage at a time that it benefitted the cause.

By September, 1938, Anderson was flying a Piper Cub and instructing the Civilian Pilot Training Program at Howard University, then a majority Black school in Washington, D.C. This put him into a position to be recognized as a potential asset and was recruited to become chief instructor in the nascent training program for Black pilots in Tuskegee. There he developed the program, taught the first advanced flight training courses, and earned the nickname "Chief".

C. Alfred "Chief" Anderson

"Chief" Anderson's contribution to the formation of the Tuskegee Airmen was overwhelming. It will be further covered in the following chapter. Subsequent to the end of the Second World War, Anderson went on training aviators of color as well as white pilots at

Mouton Field in Tuskegee. At that time, pilot training was covered under the G.I. Bill of Rights, a program proposed and designed by the American Legion with the goal of reintegrating returning servicemen into civilian careers and life.

Beginning in 1951 Anderson began training U.S. Army and Air Force Reserve Officer Training Corps (ROTC) cadets along with his private students. He went on, along with fellow Tuskegee instructor Edward Gibbs, to co-found Negro Airmen International (NAI), in 1967. The organization's mission statement says, "NAI has promoted the inclusion of African Americans in aviation activities through a number of programs, projects and education activities." These activities have included summer programs for teenagers of color to learn to fly and become involved in aviation.

Anderson died in Tuskegee on April 13, 1996. The C. Alfred "Chief" Anderson Legacy Foundation was established by his granddaughter Christina in 2012 to honor his legacy and continue his vision. Both the foundation, and the NAI remain active today

The fact that the Civilian Pilot Training Program opened up to aviators of color at all is due, in large part, to a chance encounter between a Missouri Senator and two charter members of the National Airmen's Association of America, Chauncey Spencer and Dale L. White. Spencer was the son of a family prominent in Lynchburg, Virginia. His mother, a noted educator and poet and his father, a town farmer and developer, entertained many prominent Black luminaries at their home as Chauncey was growing up. Notables like Paul Robeson and Thurgood Marshall. This gave Spencer a perspective on how things worked in the world of politics and political influence. Spencer went to Chicago to study aviation at the Coffey School and received a pilot's license from the Aviation

Institute. White did his aviation training at the Curtiss-Wright school where Coffey and Robinson were instructors.

In 1939, the NAAA organized a "Goodwill Flight" to Washington, D.C. to try to make a case for Black participation in the Civilian Pilot Training Program. Spencer and White were the aviators that took the mission on. In a rented plane, they reached D.C. after a few mechanical problems. There, they were met by Edgar Brown, the lobbyist for the NAAA, and the head of the Negro Federal Employee's Union.

Arriving at the Capitol the trio encountered a Senator from Missouri, Harry S. Truman. Brown got the Senator's attention and the group had a discussion. Form Spencer's autobiography, Truman asked what the pair did for a living and why they were in Washington. The pair told Truman that they had flown to Washington to "... dramatize the need for inclusion of the Negro in the Army Air Corps." Truman asked, "Why aren't you in the Air Corps? Can't you get in?"

Brown explained to him that Black people were excluded based only on their race. Truman asked if they had tried to join. The pair told him, "No", but that others had and were rejected. They didn't want to be publicly embarrassed as were the African-Americans that had tried. They wanted help in breaking down those barriers, though.

Full of questions, Truman wanted to know all about the flight and to look at the airplane. Truman told them that if they had the guts to make that flight, he would do likewise and support their efforts. So, that encounter cracked the door open that resulted in Black CPTP schools to be established in Chicago and at Tuskegee, Alabama.

Sadly, neither man get to fly as an Army pilot. Spencer went on to a career in government service. White, too old to apply for duty when U.S.

involvement World War II began, went to work as a mechanic at Wright-Patterson air base. Chauncey E. Spencer's son and namesake continues to carry on his legacy and work through Chauncey Spencer Educational Services and the African American Aviation Traveling Museum through the National College Resources Foundation.

CHAPTER 7 - THE TUSKEGEE AIRMEN

Much has been written about what was at the time, the bold experiment that resulted in the first U.S. Army Air Forces combat flying squadrons that would become known as the "Tuskegee Airmen". In 1939 the Tuskegee Institute in Alabama was part of a program funded by the United States government to attract African-Americans to civilian flight schools. When the United States became involved in World War I numerous Black Americans had applied to become aviators. All were rejected. Pursuant to that, the National Association for the Advancement of Colored People (NAACP) and several prominent civil rights leaders pressed the government for changes in the law so that aviators of color would be allowed, and for the funding and support to make it reality.

The Tuskegee Airmen

History will record that the experiment was a roaring success in most ways, although acceptance of Black Americans as combat aviators was slow to arrive outside of the U.S. Army Air Forces (USAAF) units that arose from the Tuskegee initiative. The U.S. Navy didn't give an African-

American wings until 1948, and the Marines took an additional four years to break the color barrier.

On the plus side of the ledger, the units that made up the Tuskegee Airmen, and their individual personnel, were esteemed for their combat prowess and flying skills. Still, it took the American military years to see Black pilots flying side-by-side with white aviators.

After taking power in 1933, German Chancellor Adolph Hitler had covertly, and in direct violation of the Treaty of Versailles, begun building up military technology. This was often done by developing aircraft and ships as commercial transports, but ones that could easily be converted to military use. Germany also formed numerous glider clubs, providing a way to surreptitiously train pilots.

In 1936, Hitler began openly defying the agreement, and was met by little resistance from France and England. By the end of 1938 the German military, allied with the Italians, had begun showing its propensity toward aggression. In 1935 Italy attacked Ethiopia with the intent of making it an Italian colony. The Rome-Berlin axis actively involved itself in the Spanish Civil War in 1936 on the side of the Nationalist rebels, giving it a theater in which to train troops and pilots in real battle conditions. The conquest of Europe began in earnest when Germany annexed Austria in 1938.

In April, 1939, with war looming on the horizon, Appropriations Bill 18 was passed by the United States Congress containing an amendment that designated funds for training African-American pilots. Initially, the money was to be distributed to private flight schools willing to train Black Americans. This was the start of the Civilian Pilot Training Program (CPTP) that would eventually lead to African-American combat pilots serving in the Army Air Corps.

The military already had units manned by African-Americans, but these were cavalry and infantry, and led by white officers. In 1941, the Army Air Corps, under pressure, formed its first Black flying unit, the 99th Pursuit Squadron. With only 124 licensed African-American pilots in the country and severely restrictive requirements, it appeared that the program was destined to fail.

In March, 1941, First Lady of the United States, Eleanor Roosevelt, a staunch defender of human rights and equality, traveled to Tuskegee to inspect the CPTP. While there, she took a flight in a Piper Cub with C. Alfred Anderson, who the students called "Chief".

Prior to her flight, Mrs. Roosevelt asked to meet the chief Instructor at Tuskegee. She said that she had been told that "colored people can't fly" but it was obvious that they could. "I'm just going to have to take a flight with you", so, over protests of her security detail, Anderson obliged. Forty minutes later, she is quoted as saying, "Well, I see you can fly alright!"

"Chief" Anderson and Eleanor Roosevelt

Eleanor Roosevelt, a trustee for the Julius Rosenwald Fund "for the well-being of mankind", arranged a $175,000 loan to facilitate construction of Moton Field, the ultimate home of the group known as the Tuskegee Airmen.

The Army had standardized tests in place already to help identify enlistees who would fit as pilots, bombardiers, navigators and observers. These measured both physical and intellectual abilities. It was directed that these tests apply equally to Black applicants. The War Department set additional standards for African-Americans covering education and flying experience to try to ensure that the most suitable were chosen for this new initiative.

On the verge of war in September, 1941, the U.S. Army activated the 99th Pursuit Squadron. 271 African-American enlisted soldiers were sent to Chanute Field in Champagne, Illinois, to learn the technical skills need to support a fighting aviation unit. Given the small number of people, and the highly technical nature of the training, the recruits were trained alongside white soldiers in integrated classes. This team became the core of the squadrons that were then forming in Alabama at Tuskegee and Maxwell Field.

African-American pilots trained under the CPTP at Moton Field moved to the newly constructed Tuskegee Army Airfield to receive advanced training, and for formation into flying squadrons. Tuskegee became the only Army base to conduct all phases of training, basic, advanced, and transition, at a single location. Initially envisioned for a cadre of 500, by mid-1942, with world war raging on two fronts, that population grew to nearly six times that number.

What happened subsequently has filled volumes. There were a series of white unit commanders who displayed varying levels of racism or support. The group, under Major James Ellison offended the local Alabamans by asserting that the military had legal jurisdiction over the soldiers, superseding civilian law enforcement. There was the order from Colonel Frederick von Kimble that racial segregation be strictly maintained leading to morale and performance issues, followed by Major Noel Parrish who was very open-minded, petitioning the Pentagon to put his airmen into combat.

Army segregation opened opportunities for African-American physicians, as up until that time there were none in the military. The need for air medical examiners was filled by individuals learning through correspondence courses. Ultimately practicing doctors were allowed to enlist as flight surgeons. Training at the Army School of Aviation Medicine at Randolph Airfield in San Antonio, Texas, marked one of the first integrated programs in the service.

In 1942, the Army had only two Black officers that were not chaplains. Benjamin O. Davis, Jr. was given admission to the United States Military Academy with the sponsorship of Illinois Congressman Oscar de Priest, then the only Black U. S. legislator. For years Davis was isolated by his classmates, spoken to only as duty required, forced to dine alone and had no roommate. Rather than cause him to become discouraged and quit, it seemed to strengthen his resolve to succeed. He was a graduate of West Point in 1941. That may be, in part, because his namesake and father, the other Black line officer, Benjamin O. Davis, Sr., was a career military man, raising in rank from an infantry private to, eventually, the first Black general officer in the entire military.

When Davis, Jr. graduated from West Point, his father was teaching as a professor of military science and tactics at the Tuskegee Institute. Davis, Sr. transferred to the New York National Guard and taught at Wilberforce University beginning in 1938, and attained the rank of Brigadier General in 1940.

Benjamin O. Davis, Jr., with big shoes to fill, graduated 35th in his class of 276 cadets from West Point. Commissioned as a Second Lieutenant upon graduation, he became only the second Black line officer in the U.S. Army. He had applied to the Army Air Corps when he was junior at the USMA, but was rejected as no people of color were being accepted into the flying corps. Instead, he was assigned to an all-Black infantry unit, one associated with the famous "Buffalo Soldiers" at Ft. Benning, Georgia, where he was not allowed entry into the Officers' Club.

After attending the U.S. Army Infantry School, he was assigned to teach military tactics at the Tuskegee Institute. When the War Department constituted the 99th Pursuit Squadron and began training pilots for the group that would become "The Tuskegee Airmen", Davis, Jr. was in the first class of rookie pilots.

Benjamin O. Davis, Jr.

The pilots chosen for the training all had fairly high levels of education, most with a few years of college and/or undergraduate degrees. Davis, Jr., now a Captain, became the first Black pilot to solo a military aircraft, and, in March of 1942, became one of the first thirteen African-American pilots to wear the wings of the Army Air Forces. By July, 1942, he was promoted to Lieutenant Colonel and put in charge of the 99th Pursuit Squadron.

The 99th sat idle for a long while as the politics and racism of the day kept them out of combat and off the promotion track. White officers came and went in staff positions because, as the commander of the USAAF, General Henry "Hap" Arnold is quoted as saying, ""Negro pilots cannot be used in our present Air Corps units since this would result in Negro officers serving over white enlisted men creating an impossible social situation."

In April, 1943, the 99th was finally considered combat ready, and was shipped off to North Africa. Its first assignment involved attacking an island in the Mediterranean occupied by the Italian and German forces. It was seen as strategic to opening the sea lanes that would enable an assault on Sicily planned for July of that year. The pilots had little practical training as they weren't in touch with experienced white airmen, and flew aircraft of an older design, the Curtiss P-40 Warhawk. The assault of the island began on May 30, and the 99th flew to support the amphibious troops beginning on June 2. The Axis garrison on Pantelleria surrendered and over eleven hundred were captured. This became a first-of-its-kind victory for air power. The 99th was issued a Distinguished Unit Citation upon arriving in Sicily after the successful invasion. This would be the first of three such awards given to the squadron over the course of the war.

Over the next few months, the Allies occupied southern Italy. The 332nd Fighter Group, comprised of the all-Black 100th, 301st, and 302nd Fighter (nee: Pursuit) Squadrons, joined the 99th at Ramitelli Airfield, on the Adriatic Coast. The group was assigned fighter escort duty along with attack missions on ground, rail and marine targets.

It was at Ramitelli that the pilots of the 332nd were able to replace their aging P-40's, P-39 Airacobras, and some P-47 Thunderbolts with the airplane that was later to be called "the finest all-around fighter ever built", the P-51 Mustang. Powered by a supercharged Rolls-Royce Merlin engine, it was faster and able to operate at higher altitudes than any of the planes it replaced. More critically, equipped with auxiliary teardrop fuel tanks, and with even more fuel carried behind the pilot, it could make the long flights required to escort American bombers deep into Germany.

Initially, the 332nd received P-51B models. It's English-designed, Packard-produced engine was rated at 1490 horsepower that could, for short bursts as needed, be boosted to 1720 horsepower. This gave the "B" model Mustang a top speed of 439 miles per hour at 25,000 feet altitude. It had a service ceiling of 41,900 feet, and a range, with drop tanks, of 1900 miles. Compared to the P-40 Warhawk, it was nearly 80 miles per hour faster, could fly over 12,000 feet higher and nearly three times as far.

Capt. Roscoe C. Brown, Jr.

Capt. Roscoe Conkling Brown, Jr. was part of the March, 1944 graduating class of Tuskegee pilots. Born in Washington, D.C., he was the son of a teacher, his mother, and a dentist who worked for, and was an official in the United States Public Health Service. Brown fit the profile for an ideal candidate for the Tuskegee initiative, having graduated from Springfield College in Massachusetts in 1943 as his class' Valedictorian.

Roscoe Conkling, from whom Brown got his name, served as a Republican Congressman and Senator after the Civil War. First elected in 1859, Conkling was an ardent supporter of President Lincoln's fight to end slavery in America and, after the war, was vocal in favor of full rights for African-Americans. A skilled orator, he took on disagreeing politicians up to and including Presidents of the United States Rutherford B. Hayes and James Garfield, over the way that civil service jobs were meted out. Conkling resigned from the Senate in 1881 over this conflict. When Garfield was assassinated later that year, however, Vice President Chester A. Arthur assumed the Presidency and Conkling was offered a position as an associate justice on the U.S. Supreme Court. He was confirmed by the Senate, but decided not to serve, believing he could do more as a legislator, becoming the last person in U.S. history to refuse a position on the court.

Roscoe Conkling Brown, Sr. was named at birth George Brown. He changed his name to Roscoe Conkling Brown in honor of the politician, lawyer and lecturer who fought for African-American rights throughout his career.

Roscoe Conkling Brown, Jr. was deployed to Ramitelli Air Base in Italy, joining the 100th Fighter Squadron as part of the 332nd Fighter Group. He was assigned as an operations officer and flight leader attaining the rank of captain. As flight leader he would be the quarterback, calling the plays his for fighters to execute.

By 1944 the red-tailed Mustangs were flying cover for USAAF. B-24 and B-17 bombers that conducted raids regularly. By then, the 100th was equipped with the newer P-51C and identical, except the plant in which they were produced, P-51D model Mustangs. While not appreciably faster or more maneuverable than the "B" model, they had the advantage of a bubble-type canopy allowing the pilot to see completely around him.

Based in Italy, they would intersect with the bomber formations coming from England as they entered hostile air space, and escort them to their destinations. As often as not, over the target, the flyers of the 332nd would hand off to squadrons from other fighter groups who had used less fuel and time and were more able to continue any engagement with the Luftwaffe.

Still, the pilots of the 332nd saw plenty of action on the way into the targets, and in getting back to the safety of friendly territory. However, in March, 1945, the relief squadron failed to appear and the 100th Fighter Squadron of the 332nd Fighter Group flew its longest mission of the war, all the way to Berlin with the bombers. Flying over the German capital at around 20,000 feet, Brown and his flight encountered several airplanes at "9 o'clock high", to their left and above their altitude. The flight was about to encounter the new German super plane, the jet-powered Messerschmitt ME-262. With a top speed of over 120 miles per hour higher than the Mustang, the odds were daunting.

On Brown's wing flew 1st Lt. Calvin J. Spann. Spann graduated from flight school at Tuskegee six months after Capt. Brown, on August 4, 1944 as a qualified Flight Officer.

Lt. Calvin J. Spann

Spann, who grew up in Rutherford, New Jersey, was not yet 20 years old when he received his wings. He grew up in a fairly large family, six children in all. He was sports minded and played football and ran track, and credited sports for his having learned the type of teamwork that would serve him, and his fellow flyers, well in the years to come. A religious man, he attended the Mt. Ararat Baptist Church growing up, and credited his faith for seeing him through the rough patches of his military service.

As a teenager and physically fit, Spann took up boxing for a time in a program set up by the pastor at his church. While he said that boxing taught him the importance of training, he quit after winning five bouts, all with knockouts, after seeing a film about head injuries and their lasting effects. Balancing sports, Spann said his favorite school subjects were math and science. He had the advantage of going to school in New Jersey, a state which did not embrace racial segregation. He is quoted as saying, "kids of all colors went to the same schools." One would be prone to think that this allowed him to see possibilities in the world that many children of color might never realize.

Living near Teeterboro Airport, the young Calvin saw airplanes regularly flying over his neighborhood. Barnstormers and exhibition flyers occasionally performed there, as well as the commercial and airmail planes that kept regular schedules. As a young man, a barnstormer offered him a ride in an airplane, but he lacked the dollar it would cost for the flight. Upset but determined, he promised himself he would learn everything he could about aeronautics and learn to fly. At school, he asked his physics teacher to explain the science of flight.

With aviation all the rage back then, model airplanes could be had as prizes in cereal boxes, and comic strip characters took to the sky. Spann said his favorite was "Smilin' Jack", a barnstorming pilot who lived new adventures in the air, week after week.

When the United States entered World War II at the close of 1941, Spann was just seventeen years old. Around him, older boys were being drafted in the military and, as the war continued, more and more of his friends and relatives enlisted. Word began to get around about the formation of an African-American flying corps in Alabama. Spann was told by many that the idea of Black pilots was absurd, or impossible, but he knew of Cornelius Coffey and Willa Brown, two African-American flyers who based themselves at Harlem Airport in Chicago.

Spann asked his high school counselor for permission to take the two year equivalency test in math and science. His grades were high enough he was able to apply for admission to the Army Air Corps. At seventeen, however, he wasn't allowed to enlist without his mother's permission. He had lost his father before his seventeenth birthday, and his mother told him that he was "the man of the house, now". Still, he said that she had faith in his abilities and allowed Calvin to enlist. In May, 1943, he got his orders to report for cadet training, a month before he was to graduate from high school.

Sitting in the railroad station waiting to board his train for Kessler Airfield in Biloxi, Mississippi for basic training, he sat a table next to one occupied by a couple of British Royal Air Force soldiers who were on their way to the British Flying School in Terrell, Texas. Spann overheard the soldiers talking about how, with the Allies taking the island of Sicily, they were on the doorstep of taking back Europe from the Germans. He recounts sitting there, sipping coffee, and dreaming about the faraway places that military aviation would take him.

Dreams aside, reality set in when, while sitting in the dining car, traveling below the Mason-Dixon Line, a porter told him to leave his seat. The porter explained, "Young man, a lot of times when the train stops at a siding, some folks will fire off a gunshot at any Negro sitting by the window".

So it was that Calvin Spann wound up at the Tuskegee Institute to participate in the great experiment that would eventually change the way white America viewed the abilities of its citizens of color.

Back in the skies over Berlin on March 25, 1945. On Brown's wing Spann's his primary job was to protect his flight leader. Spann's Mustang bore the number "11" on its flanks, while Brown sported "7". Surely a good omen for the superstitious. Lt. Charles V. Brantley and Lt. Earl Lane filled out the four-plane formation. Flying lead the Messerschmitt was *Oberleutnant* Ernst Wörner, an ace with ten kills.

As noted before, adding to the challenge was the fact that the American squadron sent to relieve the 100th failed to arrive, leaving Brown and his pilots the responsibility for protecting the bomber formation while they made their bombing run. For the Mustangs this meant they were using up fuel that would be required for the long flight back to Ramitelli. In fact, this would prove to be the longest mission of the war for the group. At 1600 plus miles, it severely stretched the limits of the P-51's range.

In Lt. Spann's graphic biography, *Boundless Sky*, he describes the mission. "We were on the west side of the formation when we encountered a formation of ME-262 under the (B-17 Flying) Fortresses. They were going to attack them from underneath." ME-262's had already encountered American fighters, but with their speed advantage, had no problem reaching their targets.

This time, however, with Spann covering, he and Brown turned toward the speeding Germans who were concentrating on the bombers ahead, and sought to avoid damage through speed alone. More maneuverable, the Mustangs allowed the ME-262 to overshoot. Brown wrote in his after action report, "I pulled up at him in a fifteen degree climb and fired three long bursts at him from 2,000 feet at eight o'clock to him. Almost immediately, the pilot bailed out from about 24,500 feet. I saw flames burst from the jet orifices of the enemy aircraft. The attack on the bombers was ineffective because of the prompt action of my flight in breaking up the attack."

Ultimately, Brown's flight would be credited with downing three ME-262's on that day. Brantley, and then Lane, took out attacking jets. In the meantime, American bombers inflicted serious damage on a heavily defended Diamler-Benz tank factory.

By the time Brown's flight reached Ramitelli, according to Lt. Spann, they had been in the air for six and one half hours, and their fuel gauge needles were bouncing off "E". On the ground, they were told that the group had earned another Distinguished Unit Citation.

On the same day, March 25, 1945, and an ocean away, The *Chicago Defender* published a story based upon information supplied by the Army Air Forces that said that the 332nd had never lost a bomber that they were escorting. Such was the mystique of the Tuskegee Airmen. This story persisted until the Air Force Historical Research Agency conducted a study in 2006 and 2007. In fact, 25 bombers were lost while being escorted by the Tuskegee Airmen. That being said, the average for other fighter escort units was 46.

On April 26, 1945, the Tuskegee Airmen flew their last combat mission. Enhancing their reputation, they downed four more German jets. On May 7, 1945, Germany surrendered and the war in Europe officially ended.

Lt. Spann recalled that they were anxious to take their skills to the Pacific Theater. P-51 Mustangs were already assigned to the Far East, escorting B-29 Superfortress bombers attacking the islands surrounding Japan, as well as the Japanese homeland. That order never came, however, as the Japanese conceded defeat and surrendered without conditions on September 2, 1945.

When the war ended the units that made up of the African-American flyers who comprised the Tuskegee Airmen were spilt up and reconstituted in various configurations remaining segregated from white units until President Truman's executive order integrated the military in 1948. At that point, Tuskegee Airmen still serving were assigned to units based on need and their qualifications, dispersing throughout the Army Air Forces, now renamed as the United States Air Force.

Postscripts:

The 100th Fighter Squadron was reactivated as part of the Alabama National Guard, 187th Fighter Wing at Danelly Air Force Base in 2007, in order to honor the Tuskegee pilots. They currently fly the General Dynamics F-16C+ Fighting Falcon.

The U.S. Army Air Corps 99th Pursuit Squadron of has become the U.S. Air Force's 99th Flying Training Squadron at Randolph Air Force Base in San Antonio, Texas. Honoring their legacy, the tops of the tails of their Raytheon T-1A Jayhhawk airplanes are painted red.

The 301st Fighter Squadron now lives on as the 301st Tactical Fighter Squadron, U.S. Air Force Reserve Command at Joint Reserve Base Ft. Worth, Texas flying F-16's.

The 302nd Fighter Squadron is now part of the U.S. Air Force Reserve Command at Elmendorf Air Force Base, Alaska.

Benjamin O. Davis, Sr. served for fifty years, from 1898 to July 20, 1948, reaching the rank of Brigadier General. He was honored at his retirement by President Harry S. Truman, who, six days later, signed Executive Order 9981 that abolished *de jure* racial discrimination in the armed forces. He passed away on November 26, 1970 and his remains rest in the National Veterans Memorial Cemetery in Arlington, Virginia.

Benjamin O. Davis, Jr. flew 60 missions in World War II in several different types of fighter aircraft as part of the Tuskegee Airmen. Flying P-47 Thunderbolts, and P-51 Mustangs he distinguished himself earning both the Distinguished Flying Cross and a Silver Star. Upon returning the U.S. in 1944, he was put in charge of the all-Black 477th Bombardment Group, a B-25 Mitchell unit stationed at Godman Field, Kentucky. Davis remained in the Army Air Forces and served at the Pentagon during the period when Executive Order 9981 was implemented, integrating the military and when the Air Force became a separate branch the same year. In 1953 he returned to combat over the skies of Korea flying a North American F-86 Saber and commanded the 51st Fighter-Interceptor Wing. Over the next two decades, Davis held numerous command and director positions both in Washington and overseas ultimately retiring from active service in 1971 as a Lieutenant General. He received his fourth star in 1998, capping over fifty years of service to his country, covering the most profound changes in history concerning military people of color. He died on July 4, 2002.

Captain Roscoe C. Brown, Jr. returned to university after the war and did his doctoral dissertation on exercise physiology. He became a Professor and Director of Afro-American Affairs at New York University, followed by the Presidency of Bronx Community College. He then became the director for the Center for Education Policy at City College New York and was a professor of Urban Education at the CUNY Graduate Center. He died on July 2, 2016.

Lt. Calvin J. Spann left the military after flying 26 missions in Europe and spending a year in the Army Reserve Corps. Unable to get a job as a pilot in commercial aviation due to his race, Spann spent a career in the pharmaceutical industry. Later in his life, he spent a great deal of time speaking at schools, churches and organizations where he encouraged young people to see that a grounding in science and math, combined with preparation and persistence, will lead them to success. He died on September 6, 2015.

(Author's note: It was at one of these presentations at Frontiers of Flight Museum at Dallas Love Field that my grandson and I first met and listened to Lt. Spann. I value the several subsequent opportunities to interact with him, and his wife Gwenelle, at the museum where I am a docent and educator. His memorabilia displayed there and his legacy give me much to teach and discuss with our students, many of whom come from Dallas schools in disadvantaged neighborhoods.)

CHAPTER 8 - "THE AZTEC EAGLES"

El Escuadrón Aéreo de Pelea 201 (the 201st Air Fighter Squadron)

An almost ignored chapter in America's involvement in World War II was the participation of Mexican fighter pilots and their crews supporting the Allied assaults on the Philippine Islands and in the Pacific theater.

In 1941, and through the remainder of the war, materiel vital to the Allied war effort was being carried by cargo ships from South America through the Caribbean Sea to American ports on the east coast of the U.S., and through the Panama Canal to ports on the west coast. To disrupt this lifeline, German and Italian submarines patrolled the area attacking shipping. With the Axis powers, Germany and Italy primarily, in control of much of the oil fields of the Middle East, the British were relying on fuel refined on Trinidad, and on the Dutch-owned island of Aruba. The oil flowed north from Venezuela and at least four full tankers were required daily to keep the production at a maximum level.

The United States had concentrated naval defenses covering the Panama Canal Zone and the Florida Strait between the Keys and Cuba. Cargo ships could rely on escort from Navy air crews flying the Consolidated PBY Catalina, as well as fighter planes. Additionally, American submarines were operated out of the Canal Zone.

The British deployed patrol bombers and attack planes to their airport on Trinidad. Most of the other islands in the Caribbean were owned by Netherlands and France, both countries that fell to German control early in the war. This left a big patch of ocean vulnerable to submarine operations and difficult to cover effectively. At one point, the U.S. provided Douglas A-20 Havoc attack planes and crews to British airfields on Curaçao and Aruba.

The steamship tanker *Potrero del Llano* had survived a torpedo attack in World War I while sailing under the British flag as the R.M.S F.A. Tamplin. Having been bought and sold several times, and having flown several national flags, she was under Italian registry in the port of Tampico, Mexico, on December 8, 1941. As the Western Hemisphere was dragged into the war, the Mexican government seized the ship, rechristened it, and gave control of it to *Petróleos Mexicanos* (Pemex), the Mexican national oil company.

In early May, 1942, *Potrero del Llano* left Tampico laden with 6,132 tons of petroleum. Sailing unescorted, but showing an illuminated *Tricolor* (the green, white and red Mexican flag) for identification as a neutral, she should have had no trouble. Off the coast of Florida, however, the captain of the German U-564, Reinhard Suhren, sighted the ship and, apparently, not seeing the eagle and serpent in the middle, misidentified the flag as Italian. Reasoning that no Italian ship should be in these waters, on May 14, 1942, he fired on and sank the Mexican ship. Thirteen lives were lost, but twenty-two survivors were rescued by a U.S. submarine and taken to Miami.

Seven days later, another former Italian tanker seized along with the *Potrero del Llano*, the *Faja de Oro* was sunk by the U-106 off Key West. Ten sailors died in the attack, while twenty-seven were rescued.

The sinkings provided the provocation that drove Mexico from neutrality to actively supporting the Western allies. On May 22, 1942, *Presidente Manuel Ávila Camacho* declared war on the Axis powers.

El Escuadrón Aéreo de Pelea 201 (the 201st Air Fighter Squadron) was comprised of 30 experienced pilots and about 270 support personnel, from mechanics to ground crew, electricians, and communications specialists. The unit was formed specifically to fly in support of Allied troops battling the Axis powers that lay behind the attacks on Mexican shipping. According to an article published in *The Los Angeles Times*, the members of this group were chosen only after careful and competitive consideration. *The Times* article noted, also, that this was a departure from the ways things had been done previously.

The decision to send Mexico's best pilots and crews to the United States for training and inclusion in the Allied war effort was made, it seems, to help bring Mexico a seat at the table when post-war alliances were sorted out and relationships developed. The U.S. Ambassador to Mexico, George Messersmith, saw the positives in this arrangement and endorsed the program to President Franklin D. Roosevelt, saying that the Mexican involvement would not contribute to "the actual need or help which such air squadrons would be to us", but would help facilitate Mexico's entry into the "modern world".

Mexico at that time had a rigid class system that was shared by many European former colonies. The military leadership nearly always came from the upper and upper-middle classes, from families with connections to the military or government movers and shakers. As expected, most of the pilots were from the upper classes. Reynaldo Perez Gallardo was the son of a state governor who, himself, had a military pedigree. He had spent time in boarding school in San Antonio Texas, putting him in an ideal situation for the mission.

Miguel Moreno Arreola became a pilot through connections with Fancixco Sarbia, a famous Mexican pilot at the time. But, Arreola came from a poor background, educated in an orphanage. He enlisted in military school at age 20 enticed by the 2 ½ Pesos he would receive each weekend. He was proficient enough that he quickly rose through the ranks and became one of the hand-picked 201st Squadron pilots.

Colonel Antonio Cárdenas Rodríguez brought his men across the border at Laredo, Texas, on July 24, 1944. Their journey north from Mexico City took days, as the group made numerous stops along the way to visit with friends and receive praise for their daring and mission. They arrived at Randolph Air Force Base in San Antonio Texas where they were put through the same medical and proficiency exams that a USAAF combat pilot or support crewman would be required to pass. For three months, they trained with Army Air Force instructors in tactics, armament and communications. They spent time at Foster Field in Victoria, Texas, as well as at Pocatello Army Air base in Idaho.

Although they trained alongside American aviators, the 201st Squadron personnel wore only Mexican insignias on their uniforms. Even while on American soil, only the Mexican military regulations, laws and discipline applied to them.

An American liaison team of three officers and several enlisted men acted as translators and facilitators for the training. It is noted that many of the American team had only a nodding acquaintance with Mexican Spanish. It is thought that miscommunication resulted in the fatal crash of pilot Crisóforo Salido Grijalva during training.

On November 30, 1944, the squadron arrived at Majors Field in Greenville, Texas, for advanced training in air combat tactics, gunnery, and formation flying. They were greeted at the outskirts of town by a sign that read, "Welcome to Greenville...The Blackest Land and the Whitest People". An American officer had to ask a local shopkeeper to remove a sign from his window that read, "No Mexicans, No Dogs". Against this background, the members of the 201st generally stayed to themselves after hours. However, pilot Ángel Sánchez Rebollo met a local 17-year old girl named Nancy Hudson. Defying her father's orders, they continued to see each other and on March 6, 1945, they eloped to Brownsville, and paid the Justice of the Peace $2.00 to marry them.

Captain First Class Radamés Gaxiola Andrade, the squadron commander, presented his airmen for graduation on February 20, 1945, and accepted the unit's battle flag. With that, the 201st was set to embark on its mission to help bring down the Axis powers and avenge the losses of its ships and fellow Mexican citizens.

Training continued right up to the time for overseas deployment. Crisóforo Grijalva was not the only pilot killed during training, as Javier Martinez Valle was killed during low level gunnery practice near Harlingen Texas.

In late March, 1945, having received additional instruction and physical evaluation at Camp Stoneman in Pittsburg, California, the squadron shipped out on the *S.S. Fairisle*, bound for Manilla in the

Philippine Islands. Upon their arrival on April 30, they were assigned to the 5th Air Force and attached to the 58th Fighter Group at Clark Field on Luzon.

In March, 1943, the USAAF. 310th Fighter Squadron was sent to the Pacific theater, equipped with a front line fighter, the Republic P-47 Thunderbolt. Prior to their deployment, the outfit was based at Harding Field near Baton Rouge Louisiana. The unit was charged with the air defense of their part of the United States, as part of the 1st Air Force, and was a source of replacement personnel for overseas deployment to other units as required. At Harding, they flew the Bell P-39 Aircobra and the Curtiss P-40 Warhawk. While both of these aircraft saw action in various theaters in World War II, they both suffered from a comparative lack of power and performance versus their primary Japanese and German competitors.

The P-47 had no such shortcomings. It was known as extremely rugged, and able to take hits and keep flying. Its 18-cylinder Pratt and Whitney radial engine cranked out 2,800 horsepower and gave the big, snub-nosed fighter a top speed of 433 miles per hour in level flight at cruising altitudes. American pilots called it "the Jug". The 201st flyers dubbed it "el Jarro". It could climb to 43,000 feet, and had a spectacular climb rate of nearly 3,200 feet per minute. Eight .50 caliber Browning machine guns gave it tremendous firepower for use in aerial combat, or against surface targets on the sea, and ashore. Finally it could be equipped with as many as ten 5-inch unguided rockets, or up to 2,500 pounds of bombs, making it an all-around threat to the enemy.

When the 201st arrived in Luzon, they became integrated with and began flying missions with the 310th in June, 1945. They flew aircraft borrowed from the American squadron, often flying two sorties per day.

In July of that year, the 201st received their own, brand new P-47D aircraft that carried the U.S. "Star and Bar" insignia, but the rudder was painted the green, white and red of the Mexican *Tricolor*.

In 2003, Captain Reynaldo Gallardo was interviewed by an American journalist while attending an air show at Gillespie Field in El Cajon, near San Diego, California. At 78 years old, Gallardo was one of, then, only seven pilots remaining from the Philippine operation. He said that the American pilots looked down on the Mexicans at first. Gallardo recounts a mission to strafe an enemy convoy along a frequently used road. After his strafing run Gallardo decided to do a victory roll, which raised the hackles of at least one of the American pilots flying the mission. "Look at that crazy Mexican!" was the talk over the radio. Offended, Gallardo challenged the Yank, although he wasn't sure who said it, to a fight behind the hangar after the sortie. When Gallardo arrived, his opponent turned out to be "three times as big and four times as heavy" the Mexican pilot was. Asked if he still wanted a fight, Gallardo told him he did. What ensued turned out to be a minor tussle. Acknowledging the Mexican pilot's spunk, the affair ended in handshakes and resulted in the two becoming friends. This, in turn, broke the ice and led to reduced tensions between the two groups of flyers.

During their time in the Pacific, the 201st flew more than 90 combat missions amassing over 1900 hours of flight time. 53 ground support missions were flown to help the U.S. Army 25th Infantry, Philippine Commonwealth, and guerilla troops attempting to drive the Japanese from the island of Luzon.

Aztec Eagles P-47 over the Philippines

The 201st lost five pilots in operations in the area. With no actual plan for replacements in place, new pilots were rushed through. Two of those were lost in training accidents in Florida, while the others were sent to Luzon. In all, the roster of pilots listed totaled thirty-six, including the two original volunteers killed in training.

On July 10, 1945, the 58th Fighter Group left for Okinawa, leaving the Mexican unit on their own. By then the Japanese air power had been reduced to nearly nothing. The 201st concentrated their efforts on ground attack and support missions. Not only did the pilots get involved in combat, but the support personnel were involved in direct fighting with Japanese troops, apparently capturing a number of them.

On August 26, the 201st flew its last combat mission of the war, leaving a record that reflected their having put out of commission around 30,000 Japanese combatants, and a swath of destruction that included gun emplacements, vehicles, buildings and ammunition dumps.

El Escuadrón Aéreo de Pelea 201 returned to a heroes' welcome in Mexico City, feted with a parade in Constitution Square, and delivered the Mexican combat flag to President Camacho.

A monument in Chapultepec Park stands for the "Aztec Eagles" of the 201st, and the unit lives on. It is based in Cozumel, Quintana Roo, flying missions ranging from interdiction to border security and search and rescue. The names of the expeditionary force pilots are on plaques that flank the ends of what *The Times* described as "the 201st's enormous, regal, cream-colored monument". A display in the National Museum of the United States Air Force also commemorates the unit and its contribution to the victory in the Pacific.

And, Ángel Sánchez Rebollo and Nancy Hudson stayed married for 43 years, and raised two children and had several grandkids before she passed away in 1986.

CHAPTER 9 - FROM WASP'S TO EAGLES TO FIGHTING FALCONS

As war loomed in Europe in the 1930's it was becoming evident the air power would take a major role in any future conflict. The growth of the airplane as a weapon in World War I had shown its potential, even though it was not decisive in that outcome. However, the terms of the armistice that ended the First World War, the Treaty of Versailles, directly addressed this potential in limiting the production and use of aircraft by the defeated combatants. Articles 198-202 of that agreement forbade Germany from having any naval or military air forces. Germany was not allowed to build any aircraft of any kind for the first six months after the conflict, and when production was allowed, it would exclude aircraft and airships "which are or have been in use or were designed for warlike purposes". Likewise terrestrial and maritime machines, tanks, trucks and ships among them.

Over the next several years the government in Germany changed, trading a *Kaiser* for a democratically elected, parliament. And, as history notes, this "Weimar Republic", for any number of reasons, both national and international, came to an ignominious end with the ascension of a nationalist, dictatorial xenophobe, Adolph Hitler. The National Socialist (Nazi) government began supporting production of aircraft and airships for civilian commercial use, knowing full well that the developing designs and technology could easily be converted for military applications. In some cases the governments of, and companies headquartered in the countries formerly allied against the Germans, were complicit, either knowingly or otherwise.

In the mid-1930's, for instance, giant Zeppelin dirigibles carrying the swastika emblem of the Nazi regime plied the Atlantic as airborne ocean liners delivering well-heeled passengers in opulent comfort between Europe and the United States. At the same time, the United States Navy commissioned the production of a number of rigid airships. The first of these, the USS Shenandoah, was built by the Navy using designs pioneered by the Germans and used in World War I to protect German shipping. It was powered by Packard engines, and was unique in using helium, rather than highly volatile hydrogen, as a lifting gas.

The second airship, the USS Los Angeles, however, was built for the Navy by the German Zeppelin Company. Airships that were to have been turned over as reparations after the war were, instead, scuttled by their German crews, so the Los Angeles was seen as a replacement for a debt owed. So, even though Zeppelin was only permitted to build civilian, passenger carrying airships, the Los Angeles was a war machine, and powered by five German Maybach engines.

The third and fourth successful dirigibles were the USS Macon and Akron. These were built by the joint venture Goodyear-Zeppelin Company, an alliance of Goodyear Tire and Rubber, with *Luftschiffbau Zeppelin*. Using German technology and German engineers, these giant flying aircraft carriers gave the Zeppelin company access emerging technology, including the use of rubber-impregnated cloth as the internal ballonets that contained the lifting gas, and advances in frame engineering and construction. These, also, were powered by Maybach engines.

Another notable example of potential violation includes General Motors (GM) ownership of the German automobile manufacturer, Opel GmbH. From 1862 until 1920, Opel produced first, sewing machines, then bicycles, motorcycles, and their first car in 1901 in partnership with the French company Darracq. As a standalone after 1907, Opel built itself into a formidable enterprise, owning over a third of the German car market by 1928. Enter GM. In 1929, GM purchased an 80% share of the company, and owned it outright by 1931. So, working up the start of hostilities on Europe in 1938, Opel and GM technology were intermingled. Opel's truck line was called the *Blitz*, a prophetic appellation as the vehicles became a staple of the *Wehrmacht* and its *Blitzkrieg*, or "lightning war". Opel produced components used on German bomber aircraft and airplane motors as one of the only companies able to work with thin aluminum. Although cooperation ended in 1940, at least above board, the company had at its disposal technology and resources that somehow managed to repatriate to GM when the war ended.

In absolute violation of Treaty articles, in 1935 Germany started production of the Junkers Ju-87, a single engine airplane called unembarrassedly, the *Stuka*. The name derived from the German *Sturzkampfflugzeug* which means "dive bomber airplane". The Ju-87 first saw service during the Spanish Civil War from 1936 to 1939, giving engineers and pilots a practical application to develop the technology and flight skills. When Germany began its conquest of Europe, the Stuka was the tip of the spear as the Nazis invaded Poland, and then marched through country after country during 1939 and 1940. Many of these pilots had trained under the guise of civilian aviation development.

This was not lost on the countries who would ally together to defeat the Germans, and the Axis powers that gathered with world domination in mind.

Realizing a need for qualified aviators, U.S. Army General Henry H. "Hap" Arnold pitched the idea of a network of civilian pilot development schools to the largest operators of aviation training in the country. Parks Air College, the Curtiss-Wright Technical Institute, and the Boeing School of Aeronautics all agreed and began to work toward a common goal. At first unfunded, the Civil Aeronautics Act of 1938 put money behind the program. President Franklin D. Roosevelt signed the act into law and announced it to the public on December 27, 1938. The Civil Aviation Authority (CAA) began developing Civilian Pilot Development Program (CPTP) schools with the goal of turning 20,000 college students per year into aviators. The program kicked off in 1939, with the government paying for a 72-hour ground school course and 30 to 50 hours of flight training.

When the Nazis invaded Poland on September 1, 1939, even critics of the program conceded the wisdom of the initiative. Suffering through the usual political turf wars, and a threat by the Army to coopt the entire program, the training provider formed the National Aviation Training Association (NATA), keeping the program open to general aviation students and preventing the military from banning civilian aviation altogether as war drew nearer.

By the time that the United States was drawn into the conflict at the end of 1941, the number of schools participating had reached into the several dozen. The programs were open to men and women, and two particular CPTPs were established at the Coffey School of Aeronautics in Chicago, Illinois, and at the Tuskegee Institute in Alabama, providing training to people of color.

When war came, Americans stepped up to aid the effort. Gasoline, needed for airplanes and vehicles, was rationed for civilian use. Categories of food were hard to obtain at home, with the supply going to feed the troops. With silk needed for parachutes, and mostly imported from Japan, fancy women's hosiery became either something to be avoided, or made from the new wonder material Nylon.

Young men across the country either enlisted in the armed services, or were conscripted. As most jobs in manufacturing were held by men, this left a considerable vacuum. Into this space came the American Woman. Women tossed off their frocks and donned coveralls and became the workforce that built the ships, planes, tanks, and ordnance that supplied the war effort. So was born the image of Rosie the Riveter.

As the war ramped up, the United States diverted nearly all manufacturing to the production of war materiel. In 1939, American aircraft manufacturers turned out a bit over twenty one hundred planes. The year after the total nearly tripled, and again, and increased each year until in 1944 it was well over ninety six thousand. When victory was declared, the total number of aircraft produced was more than three hundred thousand. All of those planes had to be test flown and delivered to the military as expeditiously as possible. After all, a bomber sitting in California was useless to a bomber squadron England or the South Pacific waiting to deliver a blow to the Axis.

Jacqueline Cochran was born Bessie Lee Pittman in the Florida panhandle in 1906. A working class child, she married Robert Cochran in 1920 and gave birth to a son. Her child died in 1925 and the marriage dissolved, but she retained the Cochran last name. Attractive and extroverted, she used her experience in Florida as a hairdresser to land a job in New York in the beauty salon in Saks Fifth Avenue. She concocted a story to support her identity as "Jackie", claiming she was adopted and hiding her proletariat roots from the public throughout her life.

Jacqueline Cochran

In New York she was positioned to meet many people of influence, including a studio executive and entrepreneur who helped her establish a cosmetic business and provided all manner of social connections. When Floyd Bostwick Odlum divorced in 1936, he and Cochran married.

Cochran began taking flying lessons in the early 1930's and was, by accounts, a quick study. She progressed from her private pilot to her commercial certificate within a couple of years, and used her aviating to promote her *Wings to Beauty* product line.

Taking on the male dominated world of air racing, she competed in the 1934 MacRobertson Trophy Air Race, also known as the London to Melbourne, covering 11,300 miles from Britain to Australia. Nine of the twenty airplanes entered managed to finish the race, while Cochran and William Pratt were forced to retire their Granville Brothers Gee Bee R-6H dubbed "Q.E.D" in Bucharest, Romania when the flaps failed. She was back again, this time solo, as the only woman to compete in the 1937

Bendix Air Race from Los Angeles to Cleveland, finishing third of eight competitors while flying a Beech "Staggerwing" biplane. In 1938 she won the race outright flying a Seversky P-35 fighter plane specially modified for civilian use.

Her activities put her in direct competition with Amelia Earhart, both of whom were fond of national recognition and publicity. Of course, both had husbands that stirred that pot, and could afford to. Earhart was committed to the cause of female aviators so supported every effort to allow women to compete on an even playing field with men, which benefitted Cochran enormously.

In 1933 the Frank Phillips Trophy Race was open to all aviators. Phillips' name may be familiar as he headed Phillips Petroleum, whose "66" signs were a familiar sight across America through the early 2000's. The company sponsored an air race in Chicago as part of the International Air Races. The Phillips Cup was a 100 mile, closed course race around twelve pylons. Flying a Gee Bee Senior Sportster, the lone female pilot, Florence Klingensmith, was flying fast enough to be headed for a second or third place finish.

A Minnesota native, the story goes that Klingensmith, who had a love of speed and was an accomplished motorcycle racer, was living in Fargo, North Dakota when Charles Lindbergh visited the city in 1927. It is said she waived at the "Lone Eagle", who failed to return her greeting. This "cheesed Florence off" and she decided then and there that she would learn to fly. And, so she did.

In exchange for flying lessons, she agreed to perform parachute jumps as part of a barnstorming exhibition. She was left unconscious by the first jump, but, undeterred she continued to learn to fly. While working as a mechanic's apprentice at Hector Field, she solicited support from local Fargo businesses in purchasing her first airplane, a Monocoupe which she christened "Miss Fargo". She received her private pilot certificate in 1929 becoming the first female licensed pilot in North Dakota.

She honed her skills barnstorming county fairs and flew in her first air race, finishing fourth. In April, 1930, she performed 143 consecutive inside loops, which would have been a world record, had a National Aeronautics Administration (NAA) official been there to witness and certify her feat. Air race competitor Laura Ingalls upped the official record to 980. Not to be outdone, in June, 1931, Klingensmith awed 50,000 spectators at Minneapolis' Wood Chamberlain Field, looping the loop for four and a half hours. When the total was certified by the NAA, she was credited with 1,078.

A couple of months later, Klingensmith, a charter member of the Ninety-Nines, won four women's races at the National Air Races in Cleveland, Ohio. At the event in 1932 she won the Amelia Earhart Trophy, presented to her by Earhart herself, and included a brand new Essex Terraplane automobile.

The Granville Brothers Gee Bee Super Sportster was a plane specifically designed for air racing, as were all of the Gee Bee models. While the stubby, single seat Sportster was the most recognizable and celebrated model that the company produced, the two seat Super Sportster embodied much of the airframe elements of the single. The "Y" model that Klingensmith flew at the 1933 Air Races started life as a test bed for a 215 horsepower Lycoming radial engine. For the races, however, a 670 horsepower Wright Whirlwind radial was fitted.

The National Air Race classes in which Klingensmith competed were for airplanes of unlimited power. She placed second in the

"Women's Free-For-All" race, and was in fourth place in the main event, flying against men. Like all airplanes of this era, the Gee Bee was a fabric covered airplane. Very likely overstressed by the extra power and speed from the big Wright engine, fabric began peeling off the fuselage as she passed the grandstands on the fourth lap. Obviously realizing she had a problem she leveled the wings and left the course, headed for a plowed field a couple of miles south of the airport. Before she could land, however, the plane nosed down from about 350 feet and Klingensmith was killed in the crash.

The crash gave the male organizers of the air races a reason to ban women from open events, and as noted elsewhere in this book, an excuse to place restrictions on the power of aircraft flown by women. In 1934, Amelia Earhart protested by refusing to fly actress Mary Pickford to the event, even though Pickford was due to open the event.

Through all of the politics and turmoil Cochran continued to push the envelope, setting record after record and keeping her name prominent in the aviation press, and on the street. And it was not just through competitive flying. As war brewed in Europe, Cochran led an effort to provide American aircraft to the United Kingdom under the "Wings for Britain" program. She is noted for having flown a Lockheed Hudson bomber across the Atlantic, and spent the next several months as part of the British Air Transport Auxiliary (ATA). She recruited other American women to join to fly missions ferrying American aircraft to the British. For that she was granted the rank of Flight Captain, the equivalent of a Royal Air Force squadron leader, or a U. S. major

In 1939, Cochran wrote to First Lady Eleanor Roosevelt with a proposal to build a flying corps of American women as part of the U.S. Army Air Forces (USAAF). She said that by taking on non-combat flying roles, more male pilots could be made available for combat missions. Of course, she saw herself as the commander of such an enterprise. At the time, there was an organization called the Women's Auxiliary Army Corps, (WAAC) that, while not having actual military status, had a head whose title was "Colonel". Cochran saw herself with a similar rank. The WAAC would be brought into the Army as the Women's Army Corps, known after as the WACs, in 1943.

After contacting the First Lady, Cochran also pitched her proposal to Lieutenant Colonel Robert Olds, who was in charge of the USAAF Air Corps Ferry Command. In 1941 Olds asked Cochran to determine how many women might be available for this sort of assignment, so she combed the files of the Civil Aeronautics Administration to build a list and flesh out her vision. This led to the proposal being kicked up to the commanding general of the USAAF, Henry H. "Hap" Arnold.

Apparently considering it, Arnold had Cochran take a group of qualified female American pilots to England to study the ATA and determine how effective it was, and how American pilots might fit in. He made no promises, but did assist in selecting seventy-six women to make up the group.

To qualify, the pilot had to have a minimum of 300 hours flight time, but many had over 1,000 hours. Training took place in Canada and, eventually, all but twenty-five washed out of the program. In March, 1942, Cochran and these pilots went to Britain and joined the ATA.

While Cochran was in England, Arnold authorized the formation of an organization to be called the Women's Auxiliary Ferrying Squadron (WAFS) to be trained to ferry USAAF planes. This group was to led by Nancy Harkness Love, a woman who, in spite of a traditional upper class upbringing, including going to Vassar, decided to become a pilot, an air racer, and, eventually, a test pilot. Cochran got wind of the appointment and returned to the United States.

Convinced the women could do much more than just ferry airplanes, based on her experience with the ATA, she lobbied Arnold for an expanded role. He authorized the Women's Flying Training Detachment (WFTD) headed by, of course, Cochran.

So it was that in August, 1943, Arnold combined the two organizations, put Cochran in charge, and The Women's Airforce Service Pilots, the WASP, was born. From that date, until December, 1944, Cochran supervised training at Avenger Field in Sweetwater, Texas.

Women's Airforce Service Pilots

During that period, 1,830 women, all between the ages of twenty-one and thirty-five, and at least five feet two inches tall, were accepted for the training. Ultimately 1,074 completed training and became WASPs.

Previous flying experience and pilot certificates were required, and many had obtained those through the Civilian Pilot Training Program in the 1930's, the same group that fed the ranks of the Tuskegee Airmen. While not all white, the WASPs were nearly so. The records show two Chinese-Americans, two Mexican-Americans, and one Native American as having made the roster. Apparently several African-American pilots made it to interviews, but like Janet Harmon Bragg, they were summarily rejected. Cochran told Bragg, "It was difficult enough fighting prejudice aimed at females without additionally battling race discrimination."

WASPs were stationed at 122 air bases across the country, and were responsible for over 80% of the ferry flights, delivering over 12,000 aircraft during their time active. These missions to deliver newly manufactured aircraft to the units whose male pilots would take then into combat meant that the first test flight of each plane was in the hands of a WASP pilot, as well as the delivery flight. These flights covered seventy-eight different types of airplane, and this meant that each WASP pilot was trained and qualified in as many types as possible. The estimate is that the WASP corps freed up more than 900 male pilots for combat duty.

The USAAF apparently got some backlash from male pilots assigned to fly the Boeing B-29 Superfortress and the YP-59 Airacomet, citing control difficulties. The B-29, when introduced, was the largest and most sophisticated bomber in the American arsenal, while the YP-59 was the first American operational jet fighter. Seeking to embarrass the male pilots to get them to stop complaining, General Arnold recruited WASPs to fly these planes publicly. Apparently that put a stop to the grumbling.

Throughout all of this, the WASP was never made part of the military. Military benefits never accrued, including those as basic as funeral expenses and transport for fallen WASP pilots, of whom there were thirty-eight over the course of the program. Eleven died in training mishaps, while the remaining twenty-seven were killed during active duty.

WASPs paid for their own transportation to training sites, their own dress uniforms, and room and board. Beginning in 1943 efforts were made to get Congress to militarize the WASP, even being supported by Arnold. A House Resolution in early 1944 died when a wave of public opinion lashed back fearing that a women's air corps would deprive male pilots of their role at war's end. In June, 1941, having seen defeat in Congress, the Women's Airforce Service Pilots program was discontinued. The final class of WASP graduates received their wings on December 7, 1944 in Sweetwater. At that ceremony, Arnold announced the dissolution of the organization to become effective on December 20. Congress refused to finance anymore activities, bring it to a screeching halt.

Files pertaining to the program and personnel were considered classified and sealed for some thirty-five years after the end of the program. The WASP had a mascot logo that they dubbed Fifinella. After the war, many in the group founded "The Order of Fifinella" and stayed in touch with each other to help each other find work in their chosen vocation. Remember that at that time, and for years later, women were not eligible for hire by commercial airlines, the place where their experience would certainly be most valuable.

When the United States Air Force was separated from the Army as its own branch of the military, it offered commissions to WASPs, 121 of whom accepted. But, while now in the active military with the accompanying benefits, their roles did not include flying airplanes.

Beginning in 1970, and over the next few years, bills were introduced in Congress to give the WASPs military veteran status. The first was introduced by Senator Barry Goldwater, who had flown with WASPs in World War II. It failed, as did bills in 1972 and 1977.

However, things improved in 1977 when the WASP files were unsealed because of an uproar over an Air Force press release that stated the for the first time women were being trained to fly military missions. General Arnold's son, Colonel Bruce Arnold, took up the cause and began waging what they called "The Battle of Congress". The G.I. Bill Improvement Act of 1977, signed by President Jimmy Carter, gave the women veterans' benefits. In 1984 every WASP pilot was presented with the World War II Victory Medal, and every one with at least one year of service received American Theater Ribbon / American Campaign Medal, also. Sadly, because of the passage of decades, many were accepted by surviving family members.

In July, 2009, President Barack Obama at the behest of the U.S. Congress presented the Congressional Gold Medal to the Women's Airforce Service Pilots. Of the 1,074 that served, only three of the roughly 300 survivors were in attendance at the ceremony. Ten months later, the entire group of survivors was feted in the U.S. Capitol by the leadership of Congress.

Putting paid to perhaps the final insult to these women, on September 7, 2016 WASP veteran pilot Elaine Harmon was granted her last request and was laid to rest in the Veterans' Memorial Cemetery in Arlington, Virginia. Until that time, no WASP had been granted that honor. In fact, overcoming this last hurdle took a huge effort by her family, 178,000 signatures on an on-line petition and legislation pushed through by Representative Martha McSally, a veteran USAF pilot, and Senator Lisa Mikulksy from Harmon's home state of Maryland, and a long-time WASP supporter. Versus thirty years prior, co-sponsors for these measures could not line up fast enough and President Obama signed the bill into law after a "whirlwind twenty weeks" of introduction, committee hearings, and everything else it takes to get a bill enacted into law.

Nearly thirty years elapsed, as essentially an entire generation of female aviators was denied the opportunity to fly a military aircraft of any kind. Then, on February 22, 1974, U.S. Navy Lieutenant Junior Grade Barbara Allen received her Naval Wings of Gold at a graduation ceremony at Naval Air Station (NAS) Corpus Christi in Texas. The daughter of a career naval officer, athletic, and a college graduate with honors, she joined the Navy Reserves in 1970 and served on the staff of the Supreme Allied Command, Atlantic at Norfolk, Virginia.

In 1973 the Secretary of the Navy announced a test program to train female pilots. Her brother was a Marine aviator and she apparently relished the challenge. She applied, and was accepted. Her first flying assignment was on the Grumman C-1 Trader, a carrier-based, twin piston engine aircraft designed as a submarine hunter and later, as an electronic countermeasures platform. She became the first female Navy jet pilot when she was assigned duty flying the North American T-39, a version of the Saberliner executive jet. Over the course of her career she also flew the Douglas R6D transport (a military version of the DC-6) but left active duty to raise a new daughter.

In 1981, with the Navy experiencing a shortage of pilots, she was recalled to active duty and assigned to train at NAS Whiting Field in Florida. On July 13, 1982 while practicing touch-and-go landings at a general aviation airport in Alabama with a student, the Beechcraft T-34 Mentor they were flying entered a sharp bank at low altitude and impacted the ground, killing both occupants.

Rosemary Bryant grew up in the shadows of NAS Miramar in San Diego, California, a place familiar to anyone who has seen the movie "Top Gun". Her father had been an Air Force pilot in both World War II and in Korea, though he died when she was only three years old in a crash in 1956. She took odd jobs to earn money for flying lessons and even washed and cleaned airplanes in exchange for instruction time. She graduated from the then brand new aeronautics program at Purdue University with a degree in aviation technology. She was nineteen years old. She went on to get her pilot and flight engineer certificates before she enlisted in the Navy, and completed her Master's Degree in National Security Strategy from the National War College in Washington, D.C.

She was selected as one of the first eight women in the Navy, along with Barbara Allen Rainey, and was one of six who graduated with her Gold Wings. In 1975 Bryant flew the Douglas A-4 Skyhawk, making her the first woman to pilot a tactical military jet aircraft since the end of World War II saw WASPs flying the P-59. She went on to get a rating in the Vought A-7E Corsair II, at the time a front-line combat carrier-based attack plane.

She married in 1980 and became Rosemary Bryant Mariner, an appropriate surname, as she went on to become the first female aviator assigned to a U.S. aircraft carrier as the surface warfare officer on the U.S.S Lexington. She went on to become the first female tactical aviation squadron commander and, ultimately, returned to the War College as a Navy captain and a professor.

When Mariner died in early 2019, the Navy honored her with a nine aircraft "missing man" flyover, performed for the first time ever by all female pilots.

Other members of that class of Naval aviators included Jane Skiles O'Dea, the first woman qualified to fly the Lockheed C-130 Hercules, and the first female Naval flight instructor. Judith Nueffer, the daughter of a World War II P-38 Lightning pilot, qualified to fly the Lockheed P-3 Orion, a four engine turboprop derivative of the Electra airliner, and still used by the Navy for surveillance, as well as the National Oceanic and Atmospheric Administration (NOAA) as a hurricane hunter. The P-3 is able to fly into storms and measure intensities. Nueffer was the first female pilot to enter the eye of a hurricane.

She went on to a long career with NASA and is a senior manager at the Goddard Spaceflight Center.

Qualified as the Navy's first female helicopter pilot, Joellen Drag was angry that women were excluded from combat roles in spite of all evidence that they were capable. At one point, she was barred from hovering on the fantail of a Navy vessel by its male captain as regulations prohibited women from doing so. Drag, along with the American Civil Liberties Union (ACLU) got the regulation overturned as it prevented women from receiving the same training as was available to men. She went on to fly in the first Gulf War, and retired from the Navy as a Captain.

U.S. Army Colonel Sally Murphy retired from active duty after a twenty-seven year military career. Though the name may not be familiar, she is a pioneer, becoming the first female Army pilot on June 4, 1974 at Ft. Rucker, Alabama.

She grew up as Sally Stonecipher in Wichita, Kansas and was the daughter of a career Army officer, spending part of her very early childhood in Germany. She attended high school in Overland Park, was a head cheerleader, and graduated in 1967. She went on to college at Kansas State in Pittsburgh, completing her Master's Degree in 1972.

In 1973 she joined the Army as part of the Women's Army Corps (WAC) and completed officer candidate school in Alabama as a second lieutenant. From there, she trained at Ft. Huachuca, Arizona in military intelligence. While there, the Army opened up aviation training to women, and she applied and was accepted for helicopter school at Ft. Rucker.

She was not just a helicopter pilot, however. Her biography shows her to have flown the RU-21, a Beechcraft King Air twin-turboshaft airplane adapted for military reconnaissance and surveillance use, and the Beechcraft C-21, a militarized Super King Air. She commanded units from company size to battalion, flying first the famed Bell UH-1 Iroquois, better known to most as the "Huey", and later the Sikorsky UH-60 Blackhawk. Her commands took her across the world, including tours in Germany and Japan.

The day after she graduated from flight school she married a fellow aviator and veteran of the Vietnam conflict, Captain Dan Murphy. Their son Sean would carry the tradition on as an officer in the U.S. Army. Captain Sean Murphy served with the 82nd Airborne Division in Afghanistan and Iraq.

Upon her retirement she was honored with a Freedom Team Salute. Speaking at the event was a current female pilot and garrison commander, Colonel Laura Richardson, who told how Murphy had paved the way for now thousands of women army aviators. Murphy departed her military career to a standing ovation.

The U.S. Air Force was slower to catch up, but finally opened its pilot training ranks and graduated its first ten female aviators as part of Class 77-08, in September, 1977. There is no firm "first" with this group, as all got their wings at the same time. Most often mentioned is an Air Force nurse who was accepted for flight training, Captain Connie Engel.

On August 26, 1976, Capt. Connie Engel, Capt. Kathy LaSauce, Capt. Mary Donahue, Capt. Susan Rogers, Capt. Christine Schott, 1st Lt. Sandra Scott, 1st Lt. Victoria Crawford, 2nd Lt. Mary Livingston, 2nd Lt. Carol Scherer, and 2nd Lt. Kathleen Rambo began the flight screening program at Hondo Municipal Airport in Texas. The training included time in the Cessna T-41 Mescalero, essentially a 172 Skyhawk, the sort of plane in which most civilian private pilots first earn their wings.

Having passed the preliminary screening, Engel and her nine sister aviation trainees moved to Williams AFB in Arizona to complete their training. In all, each student spent 790 hours in training, 210 of which was in the air flying jet trainers, first the twin engine, subsonic Cessna T-37 Tweet, and then the supersonic Northrop T-38 Talon. She is listed by Women in Aviation International as the first in her class to solo the T-41 and T-37, and to lead a two aircraft formation.

Engel received the Air Training Command Commander's Cup for her leadership and flying ability, as well as the Officer Training Award which may be why she is considered as first.

Engel's classmate, Captain Christine Schott was the first in the class to solo the T-38. Captain Mary Donahue received class Academic Award, having missed only one question on the 395 question final exam. It is recorded that all of the women not only passed the course, but excelled.

Once graduated, the "firsts" continued to rack up. Engel became the first female T-38 flight instructor, and went on to fly as chase pilot for the NASA shuttle transportation system (STS), more commonly called the Space Shuttle.

Kathy LaSauce became the first woman to be a command pilot on the Lockheed C-141 Starlifter, a large, four engine transport plane capable of carrying over 90,000 pounds of cargo, including everything from vehicles and personnel, to entire ballistic missiles, and the plane could be configured as a flying hospital.

Mary Donahue was the first female pilot assigned to the U.S. Air Force Academy in Colorado Springs, and acted as an instructor both in airplanes and in mathematics.

When the group Islamic Jihad attacked the U.S. Marine barracks in Beirut, Lebanon in 1983, Susan Rogers commanded a C-141 and evacuated many of the victims.

Christine Schott was the first woman to qualify as a pilot on the McDonnell Douglass C-9A Nightingale, and commanded the first all-female flight crew in Air Force history.

Sandra Scott became the first female air tanker commander to perform under alert conditions, rounding out the accomplishments.

Women in Aviation International notes that these women opened the door through which hundreds have followed. In fact, Major Lindsey "MiG" Giggy was the Air Group Commander of the 80th Flying Training Wing stationed at Shepard AFB in Wichita Falls, Texas, where NATO pilots train along with U.S. flyers. Major Giggy is the daughter of Connie Engel.

Women, no matter the branch of service, were not permitted to fly in combat conditions prior to 1994. The opportunity opened up when the U.S. Congress, on August 1, 1991, lifted the ban on female pilots in harm's way that dated to 1944, the ban that resulted in the dissolution of the WASP. Of course, the chiefs of the four branches of the military expressed opposition, but by then, some 35,000 women had served in the Persian Gulf and proven their ability to perform. The bill was set to take effect in the 1992 fiscal year.

Jeannie Marie Leavitt

Jeannie Marie (Flynn) Leavitt was another woman aviator who followed the first ten Air Force pilots through the hole in the glass ceiling. The daughter of an Air Force airman, she grew up in St. Louis, Missouri, then attended college at the University of Texas in Austin, earning her baccalaureate in aerospace engineering. From there she attended Stanford University in California, completing her Master of Science in aeronautics and astronautics. In college she was part of the Air Force Reserve Officer Training Corps (AFROTC)

She joined the Air Force and began training as a pilot in 1992, with the immediate goal of becoming a T-38 flight instructor. When the ban on female fighter pilots dissolved, she was at Vance AFB in Oklahoma, and applied for upgrade training for the F-15E Strike Eagle. Over the course of the next several years she became an instructor both for pilot training and in weapons systems.

In the mid-1990's Leavitt deployed to the Middle East, flying NATO coalition missions over Iraq. When Operation Iraqi Freedom commenced in 2003, she was in the air over Iraq and Afghanistan, ultimately logging over 300 combat mission hours.

In the meantime, Leavitt completed three additional master's degrees; an MBA from Auburn University, a Master of Military Art and Science from the Air Command Staff College at Maxwell AFB, and a Master of National Security Strategy from the National War College.

In 2007, Leavitt assumed her first command with the 333rd Fighter Squadron based in North Carolina, in 2012, the 4th Fighter Wing at the same air force base, and, finally, the 57th Wing at Nellis AFB. The 57th provides advanced combat training to aviators from all branches of service and is the home of the Air Force's Weapons School and, most notably, the Thunderbirds Air Demonstration Squadron, who thrill hundreds of thousands of air show attendees every year with their precision formation aerobatics and flying.

At this writing, Leavitt holds the rank of Brigadier General and is commander of the Air Force Recruiting Service at Randolph, AFB, in San Antonio, Texas.

All Marine Corps pilots are considered as combat pilots. Sarah Deal grew up in rural Ohio. She worked on a dairy farm and earned her Bachelor of Science degree from Kent State University, financed by catching, raising and selling one prize pig a year as a 4H member. While at Kent State, she got her private pilot certificate, as well as a multi-engine rating and air transport pilot certificate.

While "...hanging out at the airfield (she) ran into the Marine recruiters there." After graduation in 1992, she joined the U.S. Marine Corps, knowing she would not be able to fly. She requested a specialty in aviation maintenance and was sent to air control school. Halfway through her training she recalls seeing an article in the newspaper stating that restrictions on woman aviators was being lifted. She recounts calling Marine headquarters and telling some nonplussed colonel that was what she wanted to do. "I can't imagine what that colonel must have thought about a little second lieutenant calling up and telling him she'd read something in the newspaper."

Deal's description of her experience following her decision to go to flight school, and during the bulk of her active duty career is, by virtue of its candor, instructive. Deal was trained and certified to fly the Sikorsky CH-53 Sea Stallion heavy lift helicopter, capable of carrying 35,000 pounds, and a mainstay in the war zones in the Middle East.

"It sucked,' she says, of arriving at flight school. I was a loner. I had to be. People who had been my friends at basic were no longer my friends. There was a small group of us that had gone on weekend trips together, celebrated birthdays together. I saw one of them when I arrived at Pensacola, and said 'Hey! Let's go do something! Her friend looked at her and said 'I can't.' When she

asked why, he said 'It wouldn't be right.' She never talked to him again."

"'Nobody wanted me assigned to them,' she says. 'I found this out years later. Finally the commanding officer of my first unit said: is she a qualified pilot? I don't care if it's a man or a woman, send her this way.'"

For her first "overseas" deployment, Deal, who had trained for combat, was due to be part of a convoy from San Diego to Kuwait. At the last moment, her commanding officer reassigned her to a rear detachment command, and she stayed out of the action.

Discouraged, she left active duty status to be with her twin sons from whom she was separated by her non-overseas deployment. She transferred to the Marine Reserves. Six years later her unit was called up for deployment to the British base, Camp Bastion in Afghanistan where she "flew six or seven hour missions every day, (hauling) generators...diplomats and POW's" and, even, delivering ballots for the Afghan elections during Operation Enduring Freedom. "We kind of got used to being shot at."

She recounted being glad that at least she was now doing the job for which she was trained, even when those "six hour missions" often ran to eleven hours or more. She recounts one mission that turned into a medical evacuation, a job that she and her crew were not trained for, but they were the only aircraft near enough to the situation to be of use.

After that deployment she found assignments that would keep her home and near her family, now three kids and her Naval jet aviator pilot husband, but as of November, 2017 she was shown as redeployed to the Middle East.

Perhaps the final barrier to broken was that of an African-American female assuming the controls of a U.S. fighter plane. This fell to Shawna Rochelle Kimbrell. When Kimbrell was born in April, 1976, the first female Air Force pilots were still a year and a half from getting their wings. Her parents were from Guyana and migrated to the United States for educational opportunities and became naturalized citizens before Shawna was born. She grew up in Colorado, the home of the U.S. Air Force Academy, and expressed a desire to fly as early as fourth grade in elementary school. In fact, she says, she decided to become a fighter pilot. She told an interviewer for *DoDLive*, the Department of Defense's on-line news site, that idea of aerobatics, spins, rolls, and flying inverted really got her excited.

By fourteen, she had begun flying lessons, and joined the Civil Air Patrol (CAP). The CAP has been a resource where thousands of young people have learned to fly while contributing to society, and getting a basic feeling for the structure of a military career. She worked at air shows to earn money for her private pilot certificate.

With a Ph.D. father, her family was very committed to education as a path to success. Given her goals, Kimbrell applied for the one institution that would result in her achieving her dream, the Air Force Academy. She admits to not having a backup plan if this one failed. It did not, and she graduated in 1998 with a degree in engineering, and earned her pilot wings in November of the following year at Laughlin AFB in San Antonio, Texas. From there, she went to Luke AFB in

Arizona to train to fly the front line Air Force fighter, the F-16 Fighting Falcon, completing that course in August, 2000.

After graduating from the program at Luke, assignment took her to Japan and the 13th Fighter Squadron. While based there, she deployed to Turkey and Saudi Arabia to enforce no-fly zones in the Middle East as part of Operations Northern Watch and Southern Watch. This made her the first female pilot to fly combat missions for the 35th Fighter Wing, and during Northern Watch she became the first Black female pilot to "deploy ordnance" in combat.

Shawna Kimbrell

When the Iraq conflict began in 2003, Kimbrell served three years in various combat roles supporting Operation Iraqi Freedom. By 2016 she had logged 176 hours of combat flying, and a dress coat full of medals, including both the Air Force and Army Commendation Medals.

In April, 2016, now Lieutenant Colonel Kimbrell was a course manager and instructor for the Air Liaison Officer Qualification Course at Nellis AFB, Nevada. She retired from the Air Force in 2020. She spends some of her off time speaking to groups of children, encouraging them to dream big as she did.

"I literally see the lights turn on in kids' eyes when I talk to them when they realize that someone like me can go do something as cool as (being a fighter pilot). It's really awesome to be able to go out and talk to them and have them light up and say, 'I've heard people say that you can do whatever you want, but now I can put a face to the story and I can see that it can be done, which means I can go out and do whatever I want to do.' That is what I focus on and what I think is really important."

Things that all of these women seem to have in common are an exceptional drive to succeed, nearly superhuman persistence in the face of prejudice and discrimination, and the absolute need to get into the air. Most important is how many holes in the societal overcast that these heroic women opened up so others could fly through to find clear skies and VFR on top.

Chapter 10 - The Trailblazers

President Harry S. Truman ordered the U.S. armed forces to be racially integrated in 1948. That put a stop legally to discrimination in the pilot ranks. But, there are two kinds of segregation. *De jure*, the legal kind, is the type that can be erased with the stroke of a pen. *De facto*, on the other hand, is the kind that happens because of circumstance, and cannot be easily overcome. It is the result of a belief, whether credible or not, that change will result in awful consequences. In previous chapters we saw clear examples. For instance, WASP founder Jacqueline Cochran's rejection of a Black woman pilot's application to serve was dismissed with, "It was difficult enough fighting prejudice aimed at females without additionally battling race discrimination.". Or, General "Hap" Arnold, the commander of the U.S. Army Air Forces stating, ""Negro pilots cannot be used in our present Air Corps units since this would result in Negro officers serving over white enlisted men creating an impossible social situation."

Of course, now, people like four-star General, Benjamin O. Davis, Jr., the core around which the Tuskegee Airmen formed, might have, before his death in 2002, begged to differ with General Arnold, as would dozens of career officers of color, since then.

Born in 1926, Jesse Leroy Brown grew up in the rural south, a son of a Mississippi sharecropper. In his biography it said that young Jesse would stop everything and watch as an airplane passed overhead, declaring that someday he was going to be a pilot. A good student, and a standout athlete at Eureka High School in Hattiesburg, he graduated as the top math student in his class in 1944.

He aspired to become an architectural engineer, and chose to go to Ohio State, rather than a traditional Black school. When he was warned that he most likely would encounter prejudice, he is said to have stated that he did not intend to let obstacles like that get in his way. Thus he became the only student of color in Ohio's College of Engineering. He worked his way through school doing janitorial work and loading boxcars on the night shift for the Pennsylvania Railroad.

At college he saw a poster advertising the Naval Aviation Cadet Program called V-5 that would pay him to attend school and, ultimately, allow him to become a naval aviator. Never having given up his dream of flying, he applied. The program under which Brown applied apparently was not advertised in traditionally Black schools, so had Brown gone to a "friendlier" campus he would likely have never been aware of the program. He was told by nonplussed Navy recruiter, a Lieutenant Dawkins, that there was no way that he could pass the written exam and that, even if he managed to do so, there had never been a Black naval pilot, and that tradition would maintain.

Jesse Leroy Brown

Brown persisted until the recruiter ran out of excuses, and was given the several required exams. He passed all of them "with flying colors", including his physical. So, in 1947, Jesse Brown became the first Black man accepted into Navy flight school, and was assigned to selective flight training at the naval air station in Glenview, Illinois. This first step to the cockpit is designed as a "succeed or be washed out" hurdle, and Brown had to overcome in the face of odds not experienced by his white classmates. On the positive side, the roommate he was assigned harbored no ill will and welcomed him. That was the exception, however, and many of his fellow students hounded him relentlessly, trying to get him to resign.

His first flight instructor, Lieutenant Junior Grade Rowland Christensen told him, "You'll be flying with me while you're here. Just relax and concentrate on doing the job." With that, he took his first flight in a Boeing N2S Stearman "Kaydet" biplane. In June, 1947, Brown was one of thirty six naval cadets, of sixty six who had entered the program sixteen weeks earlier, who received their orders to report to Naval Air Station Pensacola, Florida, for advanced training.

Brown was introduced to the North American SNJ Texan on October 1, 1947, an advanced trainer with performance comparable with many of the fighter aircraft flown in the Second World War. Since high school, he had a relationship with Daisy Pearl Nix. Nix came to Pensacola and lived in a hotel room, allowing her and Brown to see each other on weekend time off. Even though it was against policy for a naval aviation cadet to be married, Brown snuck home over his first weekend and the two married, a fact that was not revealed until after he graduated from cadet training.

His final exam at Pensacola required he make five aircraft carrier landings, or "traps". Brown performed flawlessly, and was awarded his gold wings on October 21, 1948, eight days after his twenty second birthday. His graduation created a stir in the press, even landing him in the pages of *Life Magazine* for having broken "the color barrier".

Brown hoped to be assigned to a unit flying carrier-based Vought F4U Corsair, or Grumman F6F Hellcat fighters. He got his wish when he was assigned to Navy fighter squadron VF-32 stationed aboard the light carrier USS Wright.

In June, 1950, North Korean military forces staged a full-scale invasion of the Republic of Korea (ROK) to the south, overwhelming the ROK forces. In October, 1950, the squadron was transferred to the larger fleet carrier Leyte, then stationed in the Mediterranean Ocean. Pursuant to a United Nations Security Council declaration, the U.S. Seventh Fleet and the British Far East Fleet deployed the aircraft carriers USS Valley Forge and HMS Triumph, respectively, to try to blockade the Peoples' Democratic Republic of Korea (North Korea) and to support ROK ground forces who were rapidly falling back in the face of overwhelming numbers and aggression.

President Harry S. Truman ordered ground forces into Korea to support the ROK army and to try to beat back the surge from the north. The USS Leyte was, as were all U.S. carriers, placed on alert. The decision was made to replace Leyte in the Mediterranean with another carrier, and to send the Leyte's better trained pilots into the fray. With this order, Brown was headed to the Korean peninsula.

The ship had to sail west through the Strait of Gibraltar into the Atlantic. From there, it crossed through the Panama Canal into the Pacific, made port in San Diego, California, Honolulu, Hawaii, and Japan before arriving in the area of the Korean Peninsula on October 8, 1950.

Flying an F4U Corsair, Brown flew 20 missions in support of the ground troops, targeting everything from North Korean troop concentrations and communications lines to military bases. In November, 1950, the People's Republic of China joined the fight supporting the North Koreans, seriously upping the ante. At the Chosin Reservoir a few miles south the Korea – Manchuria border, an estimated 100,000 Chinse troops surrounded 15,000 UN troops, which led to Brown's squadron flying dozens of close support missions.

On December 4, 1950, Brown's Corsair took a hit from Chinese anti-aircraft fire that resulted in his engine losing all oil pressure. Brown announced his situation over the radio and found a place to land in the rough terrain, mushing the plane into the side of a hill belly first. The impact damaged the plane trapping Brown in the cockpit, leaving him unable to climb out.

Lieutenant Junior Grade Thomas J. Hudner, Jr., Bown's squadron commander, followed Brown's plane to the crash site. When he saw that Brown did not immediately leave the airplane, Hudner, against all regulations, landed his own Corsair wheels up about 100 yards from Brown's plane. He radioed for a helicopter medical evacuation and then tried to extricate Brown from his plane.

Losing blood rapidly, Brown asked Hudner to, "Tell Daisy how much I love her." By the time the helicopter arrived, Brown was dead. Back on the Leyte discussions got under way as how best to recover Brown's body. The ship's skipper, Captain Thomas U. Sisson decided, with Chinese troops surrounding the site, recovery would be unreasonably dangerous, and ordered Brown be given "a warrior's funeral". Seven Corsairs carried napalm bombs to the site and turned it into a funeral pyre under sheets of the flaming jellied gasoline.

Hudner, who might have been subject to discipline for his actions was, instead, given the war's first Navy Medal of Honor. Brown was posthumously given the Distinguished Flying Cross, and, in 1972, the destroyer escort USS Jesse L. Brown was launched, becoming the first U.S. Navy shipped named for an African-American.

Frank E. Petersen, Jr. enlisted in the U.S. Navy in June, 1950 and did extremely well on his entrance examinations. His recruiter told him he, "would make a great steward." Petersen decided that he would rather be a combat pilot, in the image of national hero, Jesse L. Brown.

Born on March 2, 1932, Petersen grew up in south Topeka, Kansas. He was placed in a gifted student program in junior high school and graduated from Topeka High School in 1949. He briefly attended Washburn College but quit to join the Navy. It was in December, 1950, following the death of Brown, that Petersen applied to, and was accepted for, naval aviator training. He graduated in October, 1952, commissioned as a Marine Lieutenant and Marine fighter pilot. He was the first African-American to become a Marine aviator.

Frank E. Petersen, Jr.

In 1953 Petersen was assigned to attack squadron VMFA-212, flying the F4U Corsair, like his hero, Jesse Brown. He would go on to fly sixty-four combat attack missions in Korea, launching from an airfield at Pyong-Taek, just south of Seoul, and operating as far north as the Yalu River, the border between Korea and Chinese Manchuria.

In the 1960's Petersen transitioned from propeller driven fighters to jets. He logged time in the Grumman F9F-6 Cougar, and the Douglas F3D Skynight. In 1968, he became the first Black Marine squadron commander, taking over VMFA-314, known as "The Black Knights". Between Korea and Vietnam, Petersen would fly over 350 combat missions, and would log over 4,000 hours in various Marine fighter and attack aircraft. He would earn a Distinguished Flying Cross and numerous other medals and honors, including upon his retirement in 1988, the Distinguished Service Medal.

Over his career, Petersen would be promoted to Brigadier General, and would command units from squadron size to an entire base. After his retirement he went on to work for DuPont as head of their aviation department.

Petersen died in August, 2015. On July 13, 2018, the guided missile destroyer USS Frank E. Petersen, Jr., DDG-121 was launched from the Norfolk, Virginia naval yard and officially christened on October 6 of that year.

While the integration of the armed services took a long period of time, it was at least hastened a bit by President Truman's executive order in 1948 that banned racial segregation. With no such central authority in place, civilian America was less motivated to follow suit. Advances were being made, such as the ruling in Brown v. Board of Education of Topeka, Kansas, that declared in May, 1954, that schools segregated by race are unconstitutional. In 1957 the U.S. Congress passed a voting rights act that mirrored Brown, and outlawed discrimination in the polling place. It was reaffirmed in the Civil Rights Act of 1960. However, it was not until the passage of the Civil Rights Act of 1964, that discrimination in employment, education and access to public accommodations was outlawed nationwide.

Marlon Dewitt Green was born in segregated El Dorado, Arkansas in 1900. Green attended and graduated as valedictorian from Xavier Preparatory School in New Orleans, Louisiana, and aspired to the Catholic priesthood. He changed directions in 1948 and joined the newly established U.S. Air Force which, like all of the services, was still segregated in its pilot ranks. When that barrier fell, he applied for, and in 1950, and earned his wings as an Air Force pilot.

Stationed in Louisiana, and now married, Green was not allowed to live with his Caucasian wife on base due to state policies of segregation. He managed a transfer to Ohio where he and his growing family could live together. His last Air Force assignment had him doing search and rescue from Johnson AFB, Tokyo, Japan, flying a Grumman SA-16 Albatross.

In 1957 Green resigned his commission in order to become and airline pilot. By then, he had over 3,000 hours of flight time in multi-engine aircraft. He applied to every private and commercial air carrier that he could, and was rejected by all of them. In one case, he managed to get an interview with Continental Airlines, apparently because he did not fill in the box on the employment application that asked for "race", and failed to attach a photo of himself. At that interview, five white pilots with less qualifications were hired by Continental, while Green was rejected.

Green filed a complaint with the Colorado Anti-Discrimination Commission against Continental. The complaint took more than three years to work its way to the United States Supreme Court, where, on April 22, 1963, the court ruled unanimously in favor of Green. The Attorney General of the United States, Robert F. Kennedy, ordered Continental to hire Green, enroll him in pilot training, and grant him back pay to his initial rejection in 1957. In January, 1965, Green began flying for Continental.

Marlon Dewitt Green

In the meantime, in 1964, American Airlines looked at the national wind sock and decided that the prevailing currents favored liberalizing its pilot hiring policy. As Green prevailed in court, an Ohio State graduate and former Air Force jet bomber pilot, David E. Harris applied to American. From American Airline's Facebook account:

Captain David Harris was the first African American in the cockpit of a major passenger airline. Harris joined American in 1964, flying the DC-6 aircraft. Harris recalls his first interview at American: "I felt compelled to tell the interviewer I was Black. He said, 'This is American Airlines and we don't care if you're Black, white or chartreuse. We only want to know: can you fly the plane?'" Harris retired from American in 1994, flying American's largest airplane at the time, the widebody MD-11

As this chapter is entitled "Trailblazers", Harris' success was due largely from Captain Green's battle to fulfill his ambitions, a role that cannot be minimized. Marlon Green flew for Continental until 1978. After his death in 2009, Continental Airlines christened one of their Boeing 737-800 airliners "The Captain Marlon Green".

The first woman to be considered a commercial airline pilot was an exhibition and racing pilot named Helen Richey. A "tomboy" born in Pennsylvania in 1909, she got her pilot's license at age 20. In 1933 she partnered with another female pilot, Frances Marsalis, to set an endurance record, remaining airborne for nearly ten full days. After winning a premier women's air ace in 1934, she managed to get hired as a copilot on Pennsylvania Central Airlines (PCA). Her first flight was in a Ford Tri-Motor, flying from Washington, D.C. to Detroit, and back, a scheduled route.

Richey's career was short-lived, however. After less than one year she quit PCA under pressure from the all-male pilots' union, and a state ruling that limited her flights to no more than three per month. She returned to the world of competitive flying and, in 1936, competed in the Bendix Trophy race as copilot to Amelia Earhart flying the Lockheed

Electra 10 in which Earhart would soon make her attempt to circumnavigate the globe.

She went on to train USAAF pilots as war loomed in the early 1940's, and ultimately joined the British Air Transport Auxiliary, the organization after which Jacqueline Cochran patterned the Women's Airforce Service Pilots in the U.S.

When World War II ended, women who had taken over myriad jobs traditionally done by American men were pressured to relinquish their gains and go back tending the home. Unable to find an aviation job to her liking, Richey is said to have become despondent. She told her sister," When a girl reaches 37, her flying days are over." On January 7, 1947, Richey was found in her apartment, dead from apparent overdose of barbiturates.

Getting from the right seat to the left has taken women a lot longer. Born in Colorado in 1939, Emily Howell decided she wanted to be a pilot when she took her first airliner ride at age seventeen. At nineteen, she was sandwiching a full time job between morning and evening flight instruction, spending thirteen dollars of her thirty eight dollar per week income. Fittingly, her job was as a receptionist for Clinton Aviation in Denver, a fixed base operation and flight school teaching everything from private to commercial courses, including all of the expected ratings. To supplement her wages she did odd jobs around the FBO, and flew at every opportunity to build hours, including as an airborne traffic reporter.

Howell had her private pilot certificate within a year. She worked her way into a position as a certified flight instructor (CFI), and eventually the FBO's chief pilot and flight school manager. She began applying for an airline pilot position at Denver-based Frontier Airlines in 1968 and continued to update her applications. She was becoming discouraged as several of her students, all male, got hired by the airline while she did not.

A regional airline, Frontier flew two-engine De Haviland Twin Otters and Convair 580 airliners. In January, 1973, Frontier finally recanted and hired Howell as a first officer, nearly a decade after men had broken the airline "color barrier". She flew for Frontier for three years, in various prop and jet airliners, and reached the left seat, and her fourth cuff stripe, in 1976 at the controls of a Twin Otter.

In 1986 Frontier folded, and was bought by People Express Airlines, which was then consumed by Continental. Howell stayed through the transitions, but left after a short time to take a job with United Parcel Service, giving her command of jet freighters, including the Boeing 727 tri-jet and the four engine Douglas DC-8 models being flown by UPS at the time. In 1986 she also was the pilot in charge of the first commercial all-female flight crew. And, she became the first female member of the Airline Pilots Association. Emily Howell Warner, retired from UPS in 1990 to become an FAA examiner.

The elevation of a Black woman to the post of pilot in charge is yet much more recent. In fact, at this writing, should you take a flight on United Airlines, you might well get your in-flight cockpit announcements from Melissa "M'lis" Ward. Brought up on the south side of Chicago, Ward was an ROTC member in high school. This resulted in her receiving a scholarship to the University of Southern California, and her Bachelor of Business Administration degree.

Diploma in hand, she joined the U.S. Air Force and in 1987 became the first Black female instructor pilot on the heavy lifting Lockheed C-141 Starlifter. She flew cargo out of Kuwait and the Middle East as part of the winding down of Operation Desert Storm.

In November, 1992, she left the Air Force for a job with United as first officer (copilot) on the three-engine DC-10. She got her fourth stripe and first officer status nine months later, and, as noted, remains in the cockpit.

Melissa "M'lis" Ward

Ward has a Facebook presence and posted what appears to be another milestone on November 27, 2018. She captained a United flight with a female African-American second officer, a first for United and, apparently a first in itself.

CHAPTER 11 - THE CONQUEST OF SPACE

Before human spaceflight became a reality in 1961, science fiction literature and films boldly predicted what the exploration of the last frontier would look like, and it seemed to look a lot like the social dynamics of the time. From *Flash Gordon* to *Forbidden Planet*, a good-looking white male saved a damsel in distress from the clutches of one or another swarthy adversary with a strange name, on a planet with an even stranger name, while preventing the wholesale destruction of Earth and/or the universe as we knew it.

Flash, in comic books beginning in 1934, in serial episodes in 1936, and later in a full-length film, rescued Dale Arden from the clutches of Ming the Magnificent of the planet Mongo whose aim was to conquer the universe. Even earlier, in 1929, Buck Rogers began protecting Wilma Deering from everything from the Red Mongols of Asia to the Tiger Men of Mars. Both of these comic strip characters spawned movie house serials, books, and retro-inspired motion pictures in the 1970's and 1980's.

Forbidden Planet finds the crew of a saucer-shaped starship traveling to a distant planet to determine the status the crew of a previous craft that failed to return the Earth. A young Leslie Nielsen as Commander John Evans succeeds in overcoming an invisible monster of epic proportions, the alter ego of the villain in the tale, and rescues the otherwise helpless Altaira Morbius (Anne Francis)

So, with this forming the archetypal vision of cosmic exploration, and with American's Cold War rival, the Soviet Union making leaps and bounds in the field, the United States ran headlong to engage in the space race with the aptly, ironically named "manned" space program. Even today, when asked to describe an "Astronaut", adults, as well as many young people with whom I interact in the course of providing education events, picture white, male "test pilot" types. And so, in 1958, when the original American astronauts were chosen for the initial foray outside of Earth's atmosphere, the Mercury Program, they were, to a man, U.S. Navy, Air Force, and Marine Corps jet fighter and test pilots.

Beginning as early as 1947, the United States started sending all manner of animals into space. With the same thinking that caused the Montgolfier Brothers to launch a duck, a rooster and a sheep in their first occupied hot air balloon, scientists had grave misgivings about the ability of human beings to survive the physical forces of acceleration and deceleration that would be required to get out of the atmosphere, the act of living in an artificial environment for extended periods, and the weightlessness that would be experienced in orbit around the Earth, and beyond.

First to fly were *drosophila melanogaster*, common fruit flies, launched in a captured German V-2 (A-4) rocket to an altitude of 68 miles (109 kilometers), well past the U.S. Air Force 50 mile and international 62.5 mile (100 kilometer) defined beginning of "space". The experiment was meant to study the potential effect of cosmic radiation once the organisms were no longer shielded by the atmosphere, and fruit flies are ideal for tracking genetic mutations as they reproduce quickly and prolifically. (Many high-school students of my generation had experience with them in biology class.) Launched from White Sands, New Mexico, the capsule carrying the fruit flies was ejected from the rocket and parachuted back to the ground with its occupants alive.

Albert II became the first primate into space, launching in June, 1949. This rhesus monkey, implanted with sensors to measure vital signs, and sedated, rode a V-2 rocket to 83 miles above the New Mexico desert, but failed to survive the descent when capsule's parachute failed. His predecessor, Albert I only succeeded to reach an altitude half way to space. Over the next several years, a legion of rats, monkeys, and other organisms including plants were shot into, or sometimes just toward the edges of, space.

During the period that the United States was launching monkeys, the Soviet Union began sending up dogs. Their program hit its peak when, in November, 1957, they put a dog in orbit around the planet. A month prior, the Soviets had put the first ever artificial Earth satellite in orbit, called *Sputnik*, Russian for "traveling companion". *Sputnik 2* carried Laika, who was never intended to return to Russia. She reached orbit apparently unharmed, based on telemetry at the time, but died soon after (a few hours or a few days, depending on which Russian archival source one uses) from overheating and carbon dioxide buildup.

The United States would not succeed in orbiting an object until early the following year, when Explorer I was launched at the end of January. And so, the "Space Race" charged forward with each side trying to gain the prestige and acclaim that came with each new milestone accomplishment. As noted, the United States, who had formed the National Aeronautics and Space Administration (NASA) in July, 1958, set its sights on manned spaceflight, and began the process of choosing an astronaut corps in October of that same year. As noted above, seven experienced military aviators were deemed to have "the right stuff", and began training for forays into outer space.

Before the United States could get its first astronaut off the launch pad, however, the Soviet Union launched cosmonaut Yuri Gagarin, a Soviet Air Force fighter pilot on April 12, 1961. That flight would nearly complete a full orbit before reentering the atmosphere with Gagarin and the *Vostok I* capsule separately parachuting to landings about 175 miles short of the Baikonur Cosmodrome, from whence it had launched.

This was a huge "win" for the Soviets, as the American program that had begun several months before the Soviet one, had yet to launch with a human being. History shows that much of this gap occurred because NASA was developing a purpose-built manned capsule, while the Soviets adapted an existing spy satellite for Gagarin's flight.

So it was that on May 5, 1961, U.S. Navy test pilot Alan Shepard squeezed into a Boeing-built, bell-shaped capsule about six feet wide and just short of eleven feet long, sitting atop a modified Army Redstone ballistic missile. Built by the Chrysler Corporation, the Redstone was first rolled out in 1953 incorporating the technology learned from the German rockets, and German scientists, captured at the end of World War II. Launched from Cape Canaveral, Florida, the Mercury-Redstone nicknamed *Freedom 7*, flew a bit over 300 miles, reaching 116½ miles above the Atlantic Ocean, before reentering the atmosphere and parachuting to a water landing north of the Bahamas.

Before Shepard flew, though, NASA launched four other Mercury-Redstone vehicles with varying success. MR-1 in November, 1960, failed to leave the launch pad after an electrical short shut down the engines. MR-1A flew successfully a month later, and the fourth, dubbed MR-DB flew in March, 1961, unoccupied but carrying the weight and equipment that would be used for the first manned flights in May and in July, carrying Shepard, then Air Force test pilot Virgil "Gus" Grissom, respectively.

The third Redstone-Mercury was launched on January 31, 1961. Beginning a year and a half earlier, a chimpanzee given the name Ham (an acronym for the Holloman Aerospace Medical Center) began training for spaceflight. He was trained to push or pull certain levers in response to lights and sounds, and his performance was timed in order to establish a baseline. Ham, clad in a spacesuit rode his rocket from Canaveral, flying 422 miles downrange and to an altitude of 157 miles. During the flight, he performed his lever activation duties with little difference in his ground- and space-based times. Perhaps more important to future missions was the fact that the capsule over accelerated and flew nearly 50 miles farther than it should have, a problem to be addressed before manned missions.

So, while monkeys, apes and dogs might fit the "Diversity" theme, there is much more to discuss on the human side of spaceflight. To begin with, female astronauts.

During World War II the United States had a policy of not allowing women to fly combat. As we have already seen, this did not keep women from aviating. The Women's Air Force Service Pilot (WASP) program saw women flying all sorts of non-combat missions, including testing of aircraft. NASA, acknowledging that women can fly, recruited a number of female candidates for the Mercury program.

They became known as the Mercury 13. The chief NASA flight surgeon for the Mercury Program was curious to see how women would fare taking the same training and testing as the chosen men. William Lovelace II and Brigadier General Donald Flickinger invited Geraldyn "Jerrie" Cobb to participate.

Jerrie Cobb and "the Mercury 13"

Cobb's father was a pilot living in Norman, Oklahoma, when she was born in 1931. He took her on her first flight in an open cockpit Waco biplane when she was twelve. By age sixteen she was barnstorming a Piper J-3 Cub around Oklahoma, dropping leaflets to announce the arrival of circuses and giving rides to earn enough money to keep herself in fuel and oil. She often slept under the plane's wing to avoid spending extra cash. At seventeen, while still in high school she earned per private pilot certificate, and took up jobs flying pipeline inspections and crop dusting, areas that her gender allowed, as no commercial airlines would hire a woman. She completed her instrument, multi-engine, flight instructor and commercial certifications in a year. By age nineteen she was a flight instructor, teaching men, and at twenty-one she made a living ferrying surplus military fighter and bomber aircraft to customer air forces worldwide.

Cobb went on to set aviation records for speed, altitude and distance while still not yet thirty years old. She was the first woman to fly in the prestigious Paris Air Show in 1959, leading to her being awarded the

National Pilots' Association Pilot of the Year, The Amelia Earhart Gold Medal of Achievement, and the *Fédération Aéronautique Internationale's* (FAI) Gold Wings Awards. The list of other trophies and awards is lengthy and impressive and included being named one of Life Magazine's "100 most important young people in the United States", only nine of whom were female.

In May, 1961, NASA Administrator James Webb appointed Jerrie Cobb as a consultant to the space program to study the future use of women as astronauts. By then she had amassed well over 7,000 hours of flight time and flown over sixty types of aircraft, although none of them were jets. She began going through the same rigorous training and testing as the seven male astronauts in the Mercury program.

A half a world away, Valentina Tereshkova was training to become a Soviet cosmonaut. Born in Central Russia to Belarussian immigrants, her father a tractor driver and her mother a textile worker. She went to elementary school, quit at age sixteen, but continued her education via correspondence courses. Politically active, she was a member of the Young Communist League, which served her well as her life progressed. She also took up skydiving at a local aero club, a skill that helped land her in the position of cosmonaut trainee.

During World War II, the Russians abandoned the quaintly Western idea that women are the weaker sex and, therefore, are not capable of performing in combat, and need to be protected. This became especially true after the Soviet Army suffered huge losses during the German siege of Russia that began in the summer of 1941 and continued until bitter weather stalled the Axis troops outside of Moscow during the winter that year. The Soviet government rethought their personnel policies, and women enlisted in droves.

While most women wound up in medical capacities, including as doctors and nurses, of the nearly half million serving, several became machine gunners, snipers, tank operators, and, notably, pilots. Marina Raskova was accepted into the Soviet Air Force in 1933. She went on to train many more aviators at the Zhukovsky Air Academy, also a first for a woman. She has been called the Russian Amelia Earhart.

When Russia was dragged into the war, a number of trained female aviators volunteered. In April, 1942, the all-female 586th Fighter Aviation Regiment saw its first combat and was active throughout the war. Two of the original 586th pilots, both flying the Yakovlev YAK-1 fighter, and then with the co-educational 437th Fighter Regiment, scored the first female ace statuses in history.

At about the same time the Soviet military formed the 588th Night Bomber Regiment. The 588th and, later, as the 46th Guards Night Bomber Regiment, the *Nachtexen* ("Night Witches", in German) crews of young volunteers, all in their late teens and early twenties, flew some 23,000 attack sorties and dropped over 3,000 tons of bombs on German positions, earning the nickname that the Germans had given them.

Meanwhile, the 125th Guards Dive Bomber Regiment flying advanced, twin-engine bombers flew 1,134 sorties and dropped over 980 tons of ordinance on Nazi positions on the Eastern Front.

With a history of women active in aviation, the Soviet Union had no qualms about training female cosmonauts. Valentina Tersehkova was one of five women selected for the program, out of more than 400 applicants. The ability to fly an airplane was not considered important, as early space shots were ballistic exercises that required no input from the cosmonaut in terms of pilotage or navigation. The Soviets were only concerned that the candidate be under thirty, under five feet seven inches tall, and weigh less than one hundred fifty four pounds (seventy kilograms). And, they needed to have parachuting experience.

Tereshkova was a public relations gem. Her father had been a tank commander and was killed in World War II fighting for Russia. He was deemed a "Hero of the Soviet Union". Valentina was the archetype proletarian, working in a textile mill. And, an avid Communist.

Training consisted of a soup-to-nuts course in astronautics, including rocket theory and engineering, training in weightlessness (one assumes similar to the U.S. "Vomit Comet" C-135 flights), isolation testing, flight training in a dual-seat MIG-15, and 120 parachute jumps. At the end of several months of training and testing, four women were graduated from the course and commissioned as junior lieutenants in the Soviet Air Force. They included Tereshkova, Irina Solovyova, Zhanna Yorkina, and Valentina Ponomaryova.

Meanwhile, back in the United States, a Marine fighter and test pilot by the name of John Glenn was launched on the third manned Mercury mission. Dubbed *Friendship 7*, the capsule rode atop an Atlas intercontinental ballistic missile, and, on February 20, 1962, made three Earth orbits.

Later that year, Jerrie Cobb was called to testify before the Special Congressional Subcommittee on the Selection of Astronauts. At that hearing, Glenn, now a national hero, said, "men go off and fight the wars and fly the airplanes," and "the fact that women are not in this field is a fact of our social order."

So, in spite of completing all of the training required of the male astronauts, Cobb and her classmates were summarily excluded from any opportunity to fly in space.

Only a few months after that, on June 16, 1963, Valentina Tereshkova, along with her backup cosmonaut, Irina Solovyova, rode the bus out to the launch pad at Baikonur. History notes that before he boarded *Vostok 1*, becoming the first man in space, Yuri Gagarin relieved himself on a tire of the crew shuttle bus. His flight went perfectly. From that point on, seeing this as a good luck charm, Soviet (now Russian) cosmonauts have followed suit Tereshkova held up the tradition, becoming the first women to do so, and then rode *Vostok 6* into space, spending three days in orbit.

It would be nineteen years before another Russian woman, Svetlana Savitskaya, would go into space, but she flew twice on *Soyuz* missions, becoming part of the crew of the *Salyut 7* space station in July, 1982, and was the first woman to perform an extravehicular activity ("space walk") two years later. She was, also the first woman ever to have logged two space flights.

And what became of the Mercury 13? In spite of the fact that they all successfully completed astronaut training, but were barred flying into space;

- Myrtle Cagel, a certified flight instructor, returned to teaching and was involved in the Civil Air Patrol. She competed in women's air racing and in 1988 she got her airframe and powerplant mechanic's (A&P) rating from Georgia Tech. She was inducted into the Georgia Aviation Hall of Fame, and given an honorary doctorate degree from the University of Wisconsin, Oshkosh.
- Janet Dietrich became, in 1960, the first woman to earn an FAA Air Transport Pilot (ATP) license. She continued as a commercial pilot until 1974 flying for World Airways, a contractor that flew

personnel and materiel into and out of the combat areas during the Vietnam War. She died in 2008.

- Marion Dietrich was Janet's sister, and like her, earned her ATP and flew charter and ferry flights. She died of cancer in 1974.

- Sarah Gorelick was an engineer at AT&T, a pilot and a member of the Ninety-Nines, the group founded by Ameila Earhart, among others. She was active in women's air racing prior to her becoming part of the Mercury 13. She also received an honorary doctorate degree from the University of Wisconsin, Oshkosh.

- Janey Briggs Hart earned her pilot's certificate during World War II and went on to become the first licensed helicopter pilot in her home state of Michigan. She qualified for the Mercury program at age 40. She was married to Senator Phillip A. Hart, but during the Vietnam War made life a little difficult for him by participating, and once being arrested for, her anti-war activities. She died in 2015.

- Jean Hixson began flying lessons in 1938 at the age of sixteen, and earned her certificate in 1940. She became part of the Women's Air Force Service Pilots (WASP) during the war, and flew as an engineering test pilot in B-25 Mitchell bombers. She worked as a certified flight instructor (CFI) after the war, and got a degree in Elementary and Secondary Education, before joining the Mercury 13 group. She went on to work on flight simulator training techniques at Wright-Patterson Air Force Base, retiring at sixty years of age as a colonel in the U.S. Air Force Reserve. She died two year later of cancer.

- Rhea Woltman, as a young woman, moved from Minnesota to Texas and learned to fly in a Piper Cub. She eventually earned ratings in seaplanes, gliders, and multi-engine aircraft and got her ATP and CFI certificates and, like many of her sister astronaut candidates, participated in air races, including the transcontinental "Powder Puff Derby". She flew glider tows and trained pilots at the U.S. Air Force Academy in the early 1970's capping off a life as a former model, and a registered parliamentarian. She kept her pilot certificate active into 2014.

- Irene Leverton was a member of the Ninety-Nines and began her aviation career by joining the Civil Air Patrol in 1944 at age seventeen. After WWII she flew as an agricultural pilot ("crop duster") and one such flight involved spraying "Tailspin" perfume over a crowd gathered to open a new airport in Chicago. Again, like many of her peers, she was involved in air racing and flew until, with 25,762 flight hours logged, retired her certificate in 2010. She died in 2017.

- Geraldine "Jerri" Hamilton, at age four, after telling her father that she wanted badly to fly, was told, "Well, if you make real good grades and you grow up and you become a registered nurse, then you can be an air hostess." She began taking flying lessons at age fifteen, without telling her parents. She became partners with, and then married, Joe Truhill. The pair, working for Texas Instruments in Dallas flew B-25 Mitchell bombers while developing the tech giant's terrain following radar. This involved dangerous, high-speed, low-altitude flying, but she was already adept at such things as she was an avid air racer. *The Dallas Observer* quotes her friend David Adair as saying, "She's like the Dale Earnhardt of the female air-racing world. She was an intimidator." She died in 2013.

- Bernice Steadman (nee: Trimble) worked at AC Spark Plugs after school to earn money for her flying lessons. She got her pilot certificate before she got her driver's license. She opened Trimble Aviation after earning the first ATP certificate given to a woman in the United States. She trained 200 future airline pilots, but, like becoming an astronaut, wasn't welcome in an airliner cockpit as a captain. She went on to cofound the Women's Space Museum now located in Cleveland, Ohio. Her autobiography was titled, appropriately, *Tethered Mercury: A Pilot's Memoir: The Right Stuff — But the Wrong Sex.* She died in 2015.

- Gene Nora Stumbough (later Jessen) quit her teaching job at the University of Oklahoma and entered the Mercury 13 program only a few days before it was discontinued. She took a job as a flight instructor and, eventually, became a sales demonstration pilot for the Beechcraft Corporation. This got her ratings in multiple categories of aircraft and conditions, and she even flew as part of a Beechcraft formation demonstration team known as the "Three Musketeers" flying, as one would expect, Beechcraft Musketeer airplanes. She met her husband at Beechcraft and eventually moved to Boise, Idaho, opening a Beechcraft dealership and a fixed base operation (FBO).

- Mary Wallace "Wally" Funk was born in New Mexico and made her first solo flight at age sixteen. After attending Stephens College in Missouri and Oklahoma State University she earned a Bachelor of Science degree in secondary education, and picked up instrument and instructor pilot ratings. She began her aviation career at age twenty. Entering the Mercury 13 program she scored higher on tests than John Glenn, although only third best among the women. After she left the program, she became the first civilian flight instructor at Ft. Sill, Oklahoma. In 1971 she became the first woman to complete courses at the FAA General Aviation Operations Inspector Academy, making her the first female Safety Inspector for the National Transportation Safety Board. With over 19,000 flight hours logged, she is still active. In 2012, she put a deposit on one of the first commercial seats to space to be flown by Virgin Galactic. She has been the subject of a biography and a PBS documentary. She has her own web site, WallyFly.com, and a full bio on the web site of the Ninety-Nines where, as with most of the Mercury 13, she is a member.

(The author had the privilege and pleasure of spending time with Ms. Funk who, as a Goodwill Ambassador promoting aviation, participated in an annual Girls In Aviation Day at Frontiers of Flight Museum at Dallas Love Field.)

As noted above, some nineteen years passed between the flight of Valentina Tereshkova and Svetlana Savitskaya. Over the time between the first and last flight of Savitskaya, the United States had stopped sending single-use capsules into space, and had, by 1981 developed and launched the first reusable space transportation system (STS), more commonly called the Space Shuttle. In June, 1983, Sally Ride became the first American woman to go into space.

Sally Ride aboard the Challenger, STS-7

The mission of STS-7 was to put several communication satellites in Earth orbit. Ride's assignment was to operate the robotic arm in the shuttle's cargo bay to deploy the payload. It also involved the first time an object was deployed and then retrieved using the arm.

Sally Ride grew up in Southern California. In school she was interested in science, but was, also, a nationally ranked tennis player. She attended Swarthmore College for a time, and then the University of California, Los Angeles (UCLA), finally doing her last two years at Stanford University in Menlo Park, California. She earned a Bachelor of Science in English and physics, and went on to complete her Master of Science in 1975 and her doctorate in 1978, studying the interaction of X-rays with the interstellar medium.

She was one of 8000 people who answered an ad that, among other places, ran in the Stanford student newspaper seeking applicants for the space program. Having been hired, she worked on the development of the shuttle's robot arm and acted as capsule communicator for the second and third shuttle flights in 1981 and 1982, which were the first to use the newly completed arm.

She flew again in October, 1984, spending a week in space, and on the same mission as Kathryn Sullivan, the first American women to perform an extra-vehicular activity (EVA, commonly called a "Space Walk"). Ride remained with NASA until 1987 and then returned to academia, first back at Stanford, and then at the University of California, San Diego (UCSD) as a physics professor. She remained active in space-related programs throughout her life, and was the author, or co-author of a number of books aimed at encouraging children to find an interest in, and study, science and technology. She passed way in 2012, a victim of pancreatic cancer.

The second American woman in space was Judith Resnik. She, as a child, excelled in math, science, languages and classical piano. She was her high school class' Valedictorian and got a perfect SAT score, the only girl to do so that year, and one of only sixteen to that point ever to do so. At seventeen she was offered a spot at Julliard, but turned it down to study math at Carnegie-Mellon University. At some point, wanting to be involved in the more practical side of technology, she switched her major from math to electrical engineering. Following her Bachelor of Science from Carnegie, she earned her Doctorate *cum laude* from the University of Maryland.

While finishing her Ph.D. she got her pilot's license. She went to work for RCA and worked on radar and telemetry systems. She came to NASA's attention based upon that work, and joined the organization in 1977. She was recruited to the astronaut corps the following year. In August of 1984, Resnik flew on the inaugural flight of the shuttle "Discovery" as Mission Specialist, the same job that Sally Ride had performed a year earlier.

Resnik flew again on STS-51-L on January 28, 1986. With her was the first "Teacher in Space", Sharon Christa McAuliffe, a 37-year old social studies teacher from New Hampshire. Thousands of people, the author included, watched in horror as a faulty o-ring holding sections of one of the solid booster rockets together burned through, igniting the liquid fuel in the primary fuel tank, and the shuttle Challenger exploded over the Atlantic.

Between Sally Ride's first shuttle mission in June, 1983, and the end of the program in July, 2011, 44 American women flew a combined 114 STS missions. Two women, each, from Canada and Japan flew on six other STS flights. By 1985 it was not uncommon to see more than one woman on a shuttle crew, becoming a trend that, with the "glass ceiling" in space shattered, continues on the International Space Station today.

However, until 1992, another barrier waited to be broken. On September 12 of that year, Dr. Mae Carol Jemison flew on STS-47, becoming the first woman of color to fly in space.

Jemison, born in Decatur, Alabama, moved to Chicago as a toddler so that her family could take advantage of greater job and education opportunities. Her mother was a teacher and encouraged her interests in science and nature. She was an accomplished dancer and said that, in her senior year in college, had to decide whether to pursue dancing as a career, or go to medical school. She says that her mother told her, "You can always dance if you're a doctor, but you can't doctor if you're a dancer."

Jemison graduated from high school at sixteen, and was accepted at Stanford University. It apparently, didn't occur to her at the time that leaving home for school hundreds of miles away was a big deal. In 1977 she graduated with a B.S. in chemical engineering and with all of the course work completed for a B.A. in African and Afro-American Studies. She got her M.D. from Cornell University's Weill-Cornell Medical College in New York, and returned to California to practice at Los Angeles County – USC Medical Center.

In 1983 she joined the Peace Corps, serving in Liberia and Sierra Leone. She had already travelled as a medical student to Kenya, Thailand and Cuba.

As a child, Jemison says that she was always fascinated with the idea of flying in space, and was sure that by the time she actually did fly, that it would be a common, everyday job. She was inspired by *Star Trek's* Lieutenant Uhura, played by Nichelle Nichols, who set an example for her when she was ten years old.

Dr. Mae Jemison

After Sally Ride, Judith Resnik, and Kathryn Sullivan flew missions, she felt that the field had finally opened up enough to warrant her trying to become an astronaut. Her initial application to NASA in 1984 was held up as the organization dealt with the aftermath of the 1986 Challenger disaster, but she reapplied in 1987 and was one of fifteen candidates accepted out of the more than two thousand people who applied. It is apparent that her varied skills and background, and her obvious determination, turned the trick. She only flew on one mission, STS-47, in 1992, as mission specialist. In communications with the ground, she began with, "Hailing frequencies open", a line that tugs at the hearts of dedicated "Trekkies".

After leaving NASA in 1993, Dr. Jemison has a list of accomplishments that is much too long and varied for this recapitulation. Just a few include teaching, writing, entrepreneurship, and even a couple of roles in subsequent *Star Trek* films. Along with her medical degree, she holds no less than nine honorary doctorates, and is still active in promoting science literacy in schools.

Two and a half months after Sally Ride became the first American woman in space, another U.S. barrier was broken when Guion "Guy" Bluford became the second space traveler of color to launch from any nation. Prior to his first mission on STS-8 during August and September, 1983, though, the Soviets sent a Russian trained Cuban Air Force fighter pilot into orbit on a *Soyuz* spacecraft in September, 1980.

Arnaldo Tamayo Méndez was active in the Cuban Student Revolutionary Movement as a young man when Fulgencio Batista was the strongman president of the island country. On the first day of 1959, with Cuban national forces routed by the revolutionaries, Batista fled the country for Guatemala, and a government was formed by Fidel Castro and others who embraced Soviet style communism and formed a strong alliance with government in Moscow.

In 1960 Tamayo Méndez completed an aviation technical course and, then, decided he wanted to become a pilot. During the next two years he went to Russia where he completed training flying Soviet MIG-15 jet fighters. Returning to Cuba, he flew missions observing American aircraft and ships who were monitoring Soviet importation of ballistic missiles onto the island, prompting what would later be called the "Cuban Missile Crisis".

He joined the Communist Party in 1967, and spent two years with Cuban forces in Vietnam. Additional military education and service saw him become chief of staff of an aviation brigade in Cuba, and in 1978 was selected for cosmonaut training in Russia for the *Soyuz* spacecraft and *Salyut* space station program.

Tamayo Méndez and a Soviet cosmonaut were launched on September 18, 1980 and spent over a week in space before successfully returning to Earth. Now a Hero of the Republic of Cuba, and a Hero of the Soviet Union, Tamayo Méndez went on to become a member of the Cuban National Assembly. Not only was he the first person of African heritage in space, but also the first of Hispanic descent.

Guy Bluford graduated from high school in Philadelphia in 1960 and by 1974 went on to earn Bachelor of Science, Master of Science, and Doctor of Philosophy degrees in aerospace engineering, from Pennsylvania State University and the Air Force Technical Institute (AFTI), respectively. He then went on to earn a Master of Business Administration from the University of Houston, Clear Lake (Texas) and the Wharton School at Penn State. He earned his Air Force Pilot wings in 1966, and wound up at Cam Rahn Bay, Vietnam. Flying the McDonnell F-4C Phantom, he flew 144 missions, 65 of which took him into North Vietnam. After his return to the U.S., he began his Masters' studies at AFTI and continued flying as an instructor pilot, having logged thousands of hours of jet time. He also holds an FAA ATP certificate.

Guion "Guy" Bluford

He was chosen as an astronaut candidate in 1979, and trained as a Mission Specialist. As noted above, Bluford flew initially on STS-8, which launched on September 30, 1983. That flight is known for conducting the first test of the Canadian-built robot payload arm with heavy objects, and for making a spectacular night landing at Edwards Air Force Base's Muroc Dry Lake in California.

Subsequently, Bluford flew again in October and November, 1985 on STS-61-A, in April and May, 1991, on STS-39, and finally in December, 1992, aboard STS-53. In total, he spent nearly 29 days in space. Since Bluford's first mission, thirteen other African-Americans, three of whom are women, flew a total of twenty-eight space shuttle missions, but he holds the highest total of them all.

What seems to be obvious today is that the barriers to becoming an American Astronaut no longer include gender, race, or ethnicity. The path still is paved through a combination of intellectual, physical and emotional determination and just plain hard work.

Take the current class of NASA astronauts, hired in 2017. Eleven are American, two are Canadian. Included are six women and five men. All of them have at least a master's degree, while five have doctorates, and one is currently in a doctoral program. Eight are in the military, six men and two women, and one is ex-Air Force. Not all have flying experience, however. Lieutenant Kayla Barron was a Navy submarine warfare officer and Lieutenant Jonny Kim, M. D. was a Navy SEAL. Robb Kulin is a private pilot, and was employed by the private space launch enterprise SpaceX before becoming a NASA astronaut. Loral O'Hara also has a private pilots' license, but did engineering work on the Alvin deep sea submersible research craft for the Woods Hole Oceanographic Institute before being selected.

Although experienced as an Army helicopter pilot, having served multiple deployments in the Middle East, Dr. Francisco "Frank" Rubio was chosen more because he was an experienced surgeon. Bob Hines learned to fly in the Air Force as a reservist and became a NASA test pilot with degrees in Aerospace Engineering. Warren "Woody" Hoburg, Ph.D., came to NASA from the Aeronautics and Astronautics program at the Massachusetts Institute of Technology (MIT), probably the most prestigious engineering university in the country.

Marine Major, Jasmin Moghbeli was a 150 mission combat pilot and is a test pilot. Zena Cardmon's education and degrees are in biology and life science areas, and she is a veteran of a mission to the Antarctic and has served on several research vessels studying deep sea organisms. Navy Lieutenant Commander Matthew Dominick, a test pilot, has degrees in electrical and systems engineering.

Rounding out the class of Americans, Jessica Watkins has degrees in geology and environmental sciences and was on the Mars *Curiosity* rover team studying that planet's makeup. Finally, Lieutenant Colonel Raja Chari studied astronautical engineering at MIT before going to test pilot school and commanding a squadron at Edwards Air Force Base.

Of the Canadians, Joshua Kutryk was an RCAF test pilot while Jennifer Sidey-Gibbons holds degrees in engineering.

Men and women, with professional and ethnic backgrounds that range from Asia to Africa to Europe, that comprise the current crop of American space travelers seem to have only three things in common; a desire to succeed and the perseverance to do the hard work to do so. And, of course, the need to fly.

Within all of us is a varying amount of space lint and star dust, the residue from our creation. Most are too busy to notice it, and it is stronger in some than others. It is strongest in those of us who fly and is responsible for an unconscious, subtle desire to slip into some wings and try for the elusive boundaries of our origin.

K. O. ECKLAND,
Footprints on Clouds

Alphabetical Index

Illustrations and photos denoted in **Bold** type

www.ingramcontent.com/pod-product-compliance
Lightning Source LLC
Chambersburg PA
CBHW051416090426
42737CB00014B/2687